DATE DUE

GAYLORD			PRINTED IN U.S.A.

"Bob Kahle brings a strong sense of order and organization to understanding the dynamics of who's who in a focus group and how to deal with each personality type most effectively. And he does this in an easy-to-digest, fun manner. While this book is an invaluable guide for those new to qualitative research, Bob also provides highly experienced researchers with new insights and ideas. An excellent teacher, he articulates things I know innately, but would never have been able to pass on to others so clearly and succinctly."

BETSY BERNSTEIN, President
Bernstein Research Group, Inc.
Harrison, NY

"Bob helps moderators, novices, and old hands alike to identify the Dominators before they dominate and gives clear and direct solutions to manage them once they start. Kahle-trained moderators deliver group insights uncontaminated by tangential group dynamics."

GREG RATHJEN
Marketecture
Atlanta, GA

"We have all encountered 'Respondents from Hell' and Bob Kahle's workshop very succinctly crystallizes the characteristics and 'characters' to watch for. Shortly after attending Kahle's workshop, I was challenged with a group having three Dominators, one Cynic and a Joker. Much to my delight, my client was most impressed with how adroitly I kept them all productive using Kahle's concepts and tips."

SUSAN THORNHILL
Thornhill Associates
Hermosa Beach, CA

"Bob Kahle, a true teacher and professional in his qualitative research career, provides readers with not just a glimpse of recognizing the bad apple, but invaluable resources for dealing with these individuals. Through his counsel, the reader will learn how to effectively manage the problem, and make all participants in the group viable and contributing members for a successful qualitative process. **Dominators, Cynics, and Wallflowers** is a must read for any serious qualitative researcher."

JOHN CASHMORE
Market Resource Associates, Inc.
Minneapolis, MN

Dominators, Cynics, and Wallflowers

Practical Strategies for Moderating Meaningful Focus Groups

Robert W. Kahle, PhD

PARAMOUNT MARKET PUBLISHING, INC.

Paramount Market Publishing, Inc.
950 Danby Road, Suite 136
Ithaca, NY 14850
www.paramountbooks.com
Telephone: 607-275-8100; 888-787-8100   Facsimile: 607-275-8101

Publisher: James Madden
Editorial Director: Doris Walsh

This publication is designed to provide accurate and authoritative
information in regard to the subject matter covered. It is sold with the
understanding that the publisher is not engaged in rendering legal,
accounting, or other professional services. If legal advice or other expert
assistance is required, the services of a competent professional should
be sought.

All trademarks are the property of their respective companies.

Cataloging in Publication Data available
ISBN-10: 0-9786602-1-8
ISBN-13: 978-0-9786602-1-5

Contents

Acknowledgments

▬▬▬▬▬▬▬ *The process of writing,* editing, and organizing this book, in collaboration with so many colleagues, has been intellectually beneficial and personally enriching. The feedback and encouragement from colleagues has been so overwhelmingly generous that my collegial relationships have been strengthened and taken to a deeper level. I owe many thanks.

Specifically, thanks to George Balch and Hy Mariampolski for review and suggestions on early drafts of the manuscript. Both spent considerable time reviewing and critiquing this work in some detail. It is better as a result of their constructive contributions and suggestions.

Much of the material for this book was developed and presented to members of the Qualitative Research Consultants Association (QRCA), both at international conferences and local chapter meetings. More than one hundred moderators have provided feedback through sharing their stories and experiences in these workshops. I thank them all, especially Pamela Blake, Mark Herring, and the entire Philadelphia chapter who treated me so graciously. Members of the Minneapolis chapter also were especially kind to provide a forum for testing new material. I also am especially appreciative of all of the qualitative research consultants from outside of North America who took the time to attend and provide feedback at the workshops, especially those at the 2006 QRCA conference.

Assembling and editing the War Stories has been a particularly enjoyable aspect of this project. Hearing moderators' stories, the handful or two that are included, and the dozens and dozens of others shared along the way, has been both illuminating and affirming. I found that in their travels many moderators have met characters similar to the ones I describe. These stories helped me hone and extend the Typology presented in Chapter 2. I have learned and am thankful that I can share their vast experiences in this volume. All of the contributors of War Stories—George Balch (again), Lynne Doner, Bob Harris, Kristin Schwitzer, Chris Kann, Jean McDonnell, Elyse Dumach, and Hy Mariampolski (again)—are cherished colleagues who I greatly appreciate.

I also want to thank the four qualitative research consultants who participated in the international panel discussion of problem participant behavior across culture held at the Qualitative Research Consultants Association's 2006 Conference. Bob Harris (again), Peter Lovett, Jane Gwilliam and Ricardo Lopez brought good humor, good stories, and a wealth of cross-cultural experiences to the panel. Chapter 6 of this book is a testament to their wisdom and experiences.

Many clients have been kind enough to let me know their thoughts about problem participant behavior in focus groups. I thank them all, with special thanks due Rob Farmer of OnStar by General Motors for allowing me to practice my craft to the fullest extent of my abilities. All of the good folks at Martiz Research who hired me for their most challenging projects provided special opportunities to polish my skills. Sincere thanks are due to Deb Davis-Lenane.

Many facilities, recruiters, videographers, and transcribers have supported me as I have moderated groups from coast to coast, seeking to meet impossible deadlines often under ambiguous circumstances. Special thanks are due to my longtime associate at Kahle Research Solutions, Maria Hunsberger, for her loyal and conscientious support on innumerable focus group projects. Marsha Pieprzyk was especially helpful with the graphics for the companion Tool Kit.

Thousands of people have agreed to participate in focus groups I moderated. They trusted the process and me so the focus groups could really work. A few nights it did not work; most of the time it did, and occasionally the group discussions were magically insightful. I thank every participant, especially those who behaved in ways that required me to work a little harder to find the gold mine of their ideas and insights.

Of course, without the invitation to write this book from Doris Walsh and Jim Madden, none of the above would be relevant. I thank them both for bringing their special skills to this project and tolerating my balancing act of writing about doing focus groups and actually moderating groups.

Thanks on a different level are due to my wife, Shawn Kahle. She has provided eagle-eye editing on this and many of the other documents I have produced over the years. Most importantly, her encouragement and unbending support allow me to reach for higher and higher goals, at the same time making me more appreciative of each step of the journey.

While many have contributed to this book, the responsibility for any merits or deficiencies is attributable solely to the author.

BOB KAHLE
DECEMBER 2006

CHAPTER 1

The Challenge of Problem Behavior in Small Groups

I lost control of the group! As an experienced focus group moderator,* it was a dreadful feeling. I was in New Jersey and had just finished another big project. That night, the group was to be a mix of luxury car intenders —people aspiring to own a Mercedes, Lexus, Jaguar, Cadillac, and the like. Unknown to me at the time, the firm that I subcontracted with made an error purchasing the sample list. They recruited all men and all BMW owners. The client approved going ahead with the group anyway. It was my job to make it all work.

These participants, all young men and "gear heads," were there to talk about their cars and to brag about their knowledge of high-performance vehicles. They were there to let me know all the things that were wrong with current models, especially my clients', and exactly what they would do if they were the engineers in charge. This might have been manageable, perhaps even productive, had the focus of the group been about cars, but it was not. I had been hired to talk with these young men about their sales and service experiences and expectations of luxury car dealerships. This is something I had done literally hundreds of times before. I knew the objectives,

*Throughout this book, I use the term **moderator** to describe the person responsible for running the focus group. I use this term because much of this book is dedicated to how to manage the dynamics in the focus group room. Still, like many of my colleagues, I prefer the term **Qualitative Research Consultant** (QRC), as it more broadly and accurately defines the range of tasks, from conceptualization of the research problem, through sample definition and screening, through analysis and report writing. True QRCs do much more than moderate. I also use the term **facilitator**. A facilitator, unlike a moderator, is seeking to achieve a specific end result. This may be the development of a strategic plan, creation of a new idea, or completion of a task.

the clients, and was very familiar with the moderator's guide. I really knew how to moderate a focus group; I had moderated thousands, and more than one hundred on this particular topic for various dealers and dealer groups. Still, I lost control.

Most groups have at least one Dominant participant. This particular group was full of Dominant participants, strident, talkative, and over-powering. They were competing to demonstrate that they knew more, had more, and were more than the other guys sitting around the table. To say we had a bit of a "testosterone challenge" that evening is an understatement.

This group challenged me for control within the first few minutes, interrupting my introduction. They let me know their dissatisfaction with the "misleading" recruitment call and all the other things we had done wrong that night. "Where's the beer?" the one quiet participant harrumphed, getting into the spirit of things, and only half kidding. This group proceeded to talk over me, ignore my questions and me. It was a raucous, rowdy, off-topic group conversation. Nothing I did could get them focused on the clients' objectives. Mercifully, the two hours came to an end and we paid these guys and sent them home. I felt beaten, like an opponent of Muhammad Ali might feel after a bout with the champ in his prime. I felt disappointed that I had performed so poorly, but really knew nothing else I could have done to make the group more productive.

When I walked into the client observation room, initially, the client observers did not say much. They had seen me moderate productive groups many times before. After an excruciatingly long period of silence, one said, "tough night," with a bit of sarcasm. "At least we know these BMW guys are focused on performance," another said, revealing what even the neophyte auto marketer already knows and hardly the qualitative insight I was hired to deliver. Finally, the lead client looked at me and said, "Tonight was the perfect example of why we can't ever trust focus groups."

I recovered from this "perfect storm" of a focus group. Years later, the clients' critical comments still resonate deep inside me. Those words inspired me to become more systematic and methodical in understanding group dynamics. I vowed to learn how to more effectively manage Dominant participants, even an entire room full of them. I committed to becoming more professional in my preparation so that I would be ready with corrective strategies no matter the type of problem behavior I encountered. I did not realize it at the time, but on that awful night in New Jersey, this book was conceived.

Since then, I have spoken with hundreds of focus group moderators and small group facilitators, sharing many tales, some funny and others sad, of groups gone bad. I have reviewed academic literature on communication styles, group dynamics, role theory, and personality theory. I have watched hundreds of hours of focus groups, some that I moderated but many moderated by others, seasoned and green alike. I have developed papers, presentations, and workshops on problem behavior in small groups for both academic and commercial qualitative researchers. I have looked back at some of the earliest literature on the "focused interview" to find that dealing with Dominant and other forms of problem behavior is hardly a new challenge, but rather one that is fundamental to the art and science of maximizing the small group dynamic.

Whether it is the guy who talks too much or the one who will not speak at all, problem participant behavior is the bane of focus group moderators and facilitators of meetings of all types. Anyone who has been asked to run a small group meeting, moderate a focus group, or facilitate a strategic planning session encounters some type of problem behavior. In this book, I take the approach that problem participant behavior is inevitable, even predictable. As moderators and facilitators, we must develop and hone techniques to effectively manage multiple types of behaviors so that we can empower everyone to have a voice, regardless of culture, situation or personalities in the room.

This book is intended to be a practical resource for focus group moderators. Focus groups are best known as a frequently used test-

ing ground for product, service, marketing, and communication concepts. Less well known, though, is that focus groups are a social laboratory for observing and understanding small group processes. It is
the lessons learned through focus groups that I seek to share with all
who want to run more productive small group discussions. In this
book, the reader will learn from the stories of some of America's best
focus group moderators.

Beyond focus group moderators, anyone who seeks to promote
open, honest, deeply meaningful communication with small groups
of people can use this book to an advantage. The qualitative researcher
who conducts focus groups, creative problem solving sessions, or
brainstorming groups as a primary part of his or her practice likely
will benefit most from the content. Facilitators of strategic plans, people who serve as board chairs, or those who lead work-group meetings will recognize the problem behavior types described. Facilitators
and moderators of all types can customize the strategies suggested for
more productive group sessions. Observers of focus groups and users
of qualitative research information also may benefit from this book,
especially the Typology of Problem Behavior in Focus Groups presented in Chapter 2 and the cross-cultural and cross-mode discussion
in Chapter 6. The intervening chapters on specific techniques may
help client focus group observers better understand the tactics a moderator uses to manage group dynamics effectively.

Defining Terms

Problem participant behavior, for the purposes of this book, is defined
as any behavior that prevents the researcher from achieving the
research objectives or that undermines a productive small group
dynamic. For those who moderate focus groups or regularly run
meetings, problem participants need little introduction. It is the
behavior of the participant that is the problem, not the participants
themselves. In spite of their bad behavior, nearly all participants have

meaningful contributions they can make to the group.

Who has not encountered the Dominant know-it-all who quickly establishes himself or herself as the self-appointed expert in the room? Who has not met the participant who holds a deeply ingrained grudge against the sponsor or concept? We have all encountered the participant who passionately disagrees with everyone and everything. We have all met the person who feels it is his or her responsibility to talk, and talk, and talk . . . and talk, and talk . . . without regard to the specific topic at hand or any effort to organize words in a meaningful manner. The issue is not to attempt to deny access to our meetings or group sessions to people who do not behave exactly as the moderator might like, but rather to use strategies so that each type of individual contribution can be maximized without stifling or unduly influencing the opinions of others.

Defining the Need

In the 1980s, 1990s, and into the new millennium, focus groups have become a mainstream technique, and an overused and misused one at that. Unfortunately, the skill of moderators to effectively ask questions, manage the complex group dynamics, and understand the results of the focus group process has not kept pace with the proliferation of the technique. Far too many people who sit in the moderator's chair have not been trained to effectively manage group dynamics. Currently, there are neither requirements for education or training, nor demonstration of competency to be a "professional moderator." The Qualitative Research Consultants Association (QRCA) has developed a statement of Professional Competencies for Qualitative Research Consultants (See Kahle, Balch, Silverman and Harris, 2003), but there are no standards or licenses that demonstrate competence.*

* The Marketing Research Association (MRA) has developed a certification program for Qualitative Research Consultants. It launched in 2005, and it is too early to discern what, if any, effect this will have on the overall professionalism of focus group moderation.

Understanding dominant and other problem behavior in groups and using appropriate methods to empower all participants is an essential interviewing skill each focus group moderator must master. It is the moderator's fundamental responsibility to "encourage individuals and groups to share their thoughts, feelings, and ideas openly and honestly." The QRCA Professional Competencies define Interviewing Competency as:

> Knows and applies interviewing principles resulting in a sense of psychological safety and rapport with respondents. Is sensitive to culture and context; recognizes and understands variables that may influence study dynamics and results (for example, education, literacy level, gender, lifestyle, socioeconomic status, race, familial status and age). Encourages individuals and groups to share their thoughts, feelings, and ideas openly and honestly, derives understanding from verbal and non-verbal subtleties, nuances, body language and other auditory and visual cues (as appropriate); understands widely differing points of view among respondents in their own terms.
>
> (Kahle et al, QRCA 2003)

Excessive domination by one or two participants may stifle the contribution of others and appear to skew the results due to the frequency, volume, or tone of the Dominant participant's comments. Other forms of problem behavior, at worst, can undermine the entire group dynamic and, at least, be a management challenge for the moderator by diverting attention from the research objectives.

The challenge of the Dominant participant to the focus group moderator is not new. In the seminal *The Focused Interview: A Manual of Problems and Procedures,* Merton, Fiske and Kendall (1956) note that one of the key skills needed by the interviewer is to keep one person or small coalition of persons from dominating the group. Others have described and categorized problem participants and the roles they play in focus groups (See Goldman and McDonald, 1984;

Mariampolski, 2001; Krueger, 1988; and many others).

Dominant and other forms of problem behavior in small groups is hardly an unusual social dynamic. Boardrooms have Dominators, as do classrooms and groups of all types. Yet, in the focus group room, researchers must seek full coverage of the topic and engender a spirit of openness and psychological safety for the group to be revealing and productive. It is for this reason that the focus group is used as a springboard for defining strategies and tactics that can be customized by facilitators of small group meetings.

Still, there is no single volume that provides a detailed description of the common types of problem behavior moderators and small group facilitators routinely encounter. There is also no guide that articulates systematic strategies and tactics for addressing these inevitable obstacles to deep understanding of attitudes, values, and opinions. Until now.

Defining the Purposes

Dominators, Cynics, and Wallflowers: Practical Strategies for Moderating Meaningful Focus Groups fills a need in small group dynamics literature. The purposes of this book are to:

- Provide focus group moderators with practical strategies, tactics, and tools to better identify, prevent, and manage problem behavior in small group discussions.

- Build the professional literature in small group dynamics so that the true value of small group processes can be maximized.

- More broadly disseminate tools and tricks of the trade to allow focus group moderators to hold more meaningful focus group discussions.

To the professional and prolific focus group moderator, Chapter 2 of this book does not reveal any groundbreaking ideas, but rather reintroduces and classifies a set of familiar faces. A careful categorization and identification of ten common types of problem behavior is presented in Part I. This Typology of Problem Behavior has been created to help moderators identify problems early in the process so that they can anticipate the type of behavior problems they will encounter and, in turn, be prepared to manage them effectively. Often, group moderators are so focused on achieving the client or project objectives that they miss early signs of problem participant behavior. This is why understanding and using the Typology as a moderating tool can improve recognition of problem participant behavior and moderator interventions, and ultimately, dramatically and systematically enhance the learning from groups.

In the subsequent chapters, early identification (Chapter 3), prevention (Chapter 4), and management strategies (Chapter 5) are discussed and associated conceptual tools are provided.

Chapter 6 focuses on comparing and contrasting problem behavior in small groups across culture and modes of research (face-to-face, online, and telephone groups). A summary of an international panel discussion comparing problem types is presented. Four well-known moderators representing African-American, Latino, and British perspectives talk about their experiences and lessons learned with the problem types around the United States and the world.

In the effort to make this book useful and practical, a Tool Kit accompanies it. The Tool Kit is a series of laminated charts and schematics, including the Typology, cues and clues to identify problem behavior, key phrases to use in establishing ground rules to prevent each type of behavior, and management strategies for each problem type. The Tool Kit has been prepared for moderators to use as they prepare for and conduct groups, but it also can be used with client observers to inform them about problem participant behaviors and strategies to channel it.

Throughout the book, there are a series of sidebars—tales from the trenches. These real life stories are written by some of the most experienced and well-respected moderators in the profession. Beyond the sometimes humorous, sometimes embarrassing situations, these trusted colleagues relate key lessons learned from the "behavior from hell" that each of them has encountered. These stories will help many moderators learn from the lessons already suffered by others.

Read about Bob Harris's experience with a participant who was particularly hostile. This "War Story," a part of the oral history of qualitative researchers for a long time, is documented in writing here for all to read. George Balch and Lynne Doner relate two tales of "truth cops," very instructive stories about the challenge of participants who proselytize. Jean McDonnell reports that domineering participants are not limited to adult focus groups. Hy Mariampolski shares his definition of the "Rabbi," a specific subtype of Dominant respondent, who is neither problematic nor in need of "control." Elyse Dumach reflects on her early career encounter with a drunken doctor. Kristin Schwitzer shares the story of her encounter with a group of "tough guys gone wild," and describes how she handled it. I share additional stories about some of most challenging encounters with difficult participant behavior, including "Feel," the Joker. Chris Kann addresses a key problem for many moderators—curtailing blathering behavior. These stories, and the lessons learned from these experiences, provide readers with real-life examples of encounters with problem behavior and what to do about it.

This book is to be used and reused. Moderators should read it, but then come back to it (especially the Tool Kit), and customize the strategies and tactics specific to the moderator's style, the clients' needs, and the overall context of focus groups regularly conducted.

The Nightmare Respondent: Dominant, Hostile, and Intoxicated

J. Robert Harris
JRH Marketing Services, New York

THIS STORY may sound unlikely but every word is true.

I was doing a focus group for a malt liquor client. Malt liquor is a low-quality, inexpensive, malt-based alcoholic beverage that is popular among downscale, inner-city young men who drink it primarily for the cheap buzz it provides.

The respondents filed in. Collectively, they looked sullen, suspicious, and uncomfortable in the conference-room setting. One guy in particular looked really out of it; he had an aggressive demeanor and his eyes were pink and glassy. I could not believe he made it through the facility check-in procedure without attracting the staff's attention. Nevertheless, I had interviewed men like this before and was not initially troubled.

In situations like this, my opening remarks are especially important. The four-minute introduction is specifically tailored to make the participants comfortable with their surroundings, to be honest with them about the topic and what we are going to do, to assure them that their opinions are important, and to put them at ease with the two-way mirror. I try to bond with them around the job at hand, while simultaneously establishing my position as the group's leader. I finished outlining the ground rules and everything seemed fine, so I started going around the room with respondent introductions. When I got to Cletis, all hell started to break loose.

He would not say his name (although it was on the name card), and insisted that everyone call him "X." Then, in a threatening voice, he loudly demanded to know who was behind the mirror. I answered him patiently but he just got angrier. An uneasy mood settled over the room.

When the discussion finally started, he frequently interrupted and made scathing, disparaging comments about what the other participants were saying. When I asked him a direct question, he either rambled incoherently or told me that the question was too stupid to answer. Within a few minutes, the rest of the respondents, as tough as they were, were reluctant to say anything. The situation was getting out of control and I had to do something. I dispensed with the usual, "you have a phone call" routine to get rid of him. Instead, I told him point blank that we could no longer do our job with him in the room, and that he would be paid but would have to leave immediately. Things then took a turn for the worse. Mr. X angrily informed me that he was not leaving and that neither I nor anyone else was going to kick him out. To emphasize his point, he pulled his shirt aside to show us a pistol protruding from the waist of his pants.

The room went into shock. Nobody moved. At that moment, there was a timid knock on the door, which eased open just enough to allow a note to flutter in and land on the floor. The note read: "Bob, can you come outside for a second?" I put it in my pocket, walked back to my seat, then sat down and calmly said to the group, "Maybe it's my hair style (I am bald), but this is the third group I've done this week where somebody's pulled a gun on me." The entire room of players and street hustlers, including Mr. X, broke into hearty laughter. The tension was broken.

I then seized the moment and asked the respondents how we could resolve the situation. One man spoke up and said that everyone in the room was basically a good person and it was a shame we couldn't sit for two hours and take care of business without somebody messing things up. The others, now emboldened, nodded in agreement as another respondent spoke to X, "Why are you doing this? Bob's been straight with you and you've made us all look bad. Why don't you either sit down and shut up, or leave?"

In response, X quietly apologized to the group. He also asked if he could stay and help get the job done. I stepped in and told him that he could stay only on condition that he not interrupt the conversation, that he give me a brief but truthful answer if I should call on him, and that if he was uncooperative again he would have to leave. He promised the group that he would behave; we resumed the discussion, and finished the session without further incident. My terrified clients were not only happy to be alive, but were amazed that the group was salvaged and all of the topics covered.

Lessons Learned

1. Make sure the facility staff alerts you about a potentially troublesome respondent before the group begins so that this type of problem can be avoided.

2. Be very honest with your participants right from the start. Tell them what you are going to do and what you expect from them. Establish an environment of mutual respect and commitment to do what was expected. This will serve you well if a problem occurs later.

3. When you encounter a troublesome respondent, don't panic. Maintain your sense of leadership and authority. Stay calm and give the respondent every opportunity to back down and resume normal behavior. Also, try to refrain from leaving the room in the midst of a conflict.

4. If the respondent continues to cause trouble, it is often possible to enlist the help of the other participants to find a way to salvage the session. There is a natural tendency in group behavior to want to resolve an uncomfortable situation. Use it.

5. Stay focused. Don't take anything personally. Make everyone aware that all you want to do is get the job done and suggest that everyone needs to come together to make that happen.

In a situation like this one, it probably helps if you were raised in a big city, as I was, and are not easily intimidated by erratic or rude behavior. Nevertheless, while this was an obviously bizarre series of events, I believe that the above guidelines would be effective in managing most incidents of problem behavior in focus groups.

The Blatherer

Chris Kann
CSK Marketing, Inc., Racine, WI

I WAS DOING RESEARCH in a rural county with landowners who had woods on their property. Their county had become a tourist destination, creating a precipitous increase in property values and lots of pressure from developers for landowners to sell. Some of the long-term residents of the area had owned the land for generations and this sudden increased interest in their land had them a bit suspicious.

Our goal was to find out what kind of help the landowners needed or wanted from foresters, regardless of whether they wanted to use the land for recreation, hunting, or just privacy. I gave the recruiter very specific instructions on how to reduce the chance that the biggest curmudgeons of the county would end up in these groups. What I could not have coached him on was the likelihood that there were "keepers of the history" of the region who would feel compelled to share all the intimate details of that history.

We intentionally recruited smaller groups in order to build an atmosphere of trust between the landowners and the moderator. The nearest focus group facility was more than two hours away, so we held the groups in the conference room of the local fire station. This created a casual atmosphere, but it also meant that my client had to sit in the back of the room so that he could observe the discussions, as well as run interference in the hallway with the succeeding groups.

About two groups into the project, I met Marty, a man who lived on more than 60 acres of woodlands that had been in his family for over a century. He had lived in the county his whole life. "What a find," I thought. "He will know so much history of the area." However, what quickly became apparent was that he knew the history of the land owned by each of the group's participants and felt an obligation to share that, as well as every other piece of county history he could come up with in the 90 minutes of the group.

At the beginning, the respondents bonded well, enjoyed meeting each other, and shared stories about how they came to be on their land. We were building the trust that I had hoped we would among the respondents. When Marty told some stories about his history on his property, many of the newer residents were fascinated to understand and appreciate more about the area. The stories were interesting and quaint, but did not help us understand the goals these residents had for their land and how forestry could help them.

Marty also was suspicious about the goals of anyone interested in his land. Because he had by now established himself as a bit of an expert among the respondents, their responses began to reflect his suspicions. I soon realized that I was going to have to be more aggressive in keeping Marty on track and keeping his stories to a minimum.

What worked was a series of very gentle interruptions into the next few stories Marty began to tell, reminding him to "Tell me what kind of information you might want from the foresters to help manage that problem." It was subtle and did not discourage him, but got us back to the questions the client had. I also called on him less, and tried to use language that would make the other respondents feel more confident that their opinions also were valid even though they had lived in the county for less time.

Lesson Learned

After the group, the client expressed his admiration for my ability to interrupt Marty and get him back on track in such a subtle way. I was reminded that I was not the only one annoyed by a blathering respondent. The client and the other respondents are usually waiting and hoping that someone will get the Blatherer to stop rambling. Though it is a bit awkward to interrupt and redirect respondents, there are situations where the group will be lost if you don't. Having a staple of standard phrases that can be used to subtly redirect a respondent is critical in these situations. A softly raised hand and the phrase "This is wonderful information, but I want to make sure that everyone has a chance to share tonight," will take you a long way in keeping the group on track and will help you accomplish your research objectives.

CHAPTER 2

The Typology of Problem Behavior in Focus Groups

Problem behavior in focus groups is defined as behavior that poses an obstacle to the group achieving its research objectives. Problem behavior in focus groups is typically a matter of degree, from mild to extreme. Nearly every focus group contains some participants who may be more or less cooperative or who follow the ground rules to varying degrees. This chapter describes, defines, and classifies the problem behavior of participants when it rises to the point of being counterproductive to the group dynamic and poses an obstacle to achieving the group's objectives.

Unmanaged problem behavior is a threat to validity of small group research or other task-oriented processes. In cases where one or more participants overwhelm the proceedings with his or her comments, inevitably, others' opinions are devalued or even stifled. Lack of respect among participants can undermine group decorum and influence the outcome of the group. Left alone, problem behavior can result in misinformation for the client observers and less than satisfactory experiences for the participants.

This Typology of Problem Behavior in Focus Groups (see Figure 2.1) was created in the tradition of Max Weber's "ideal type." In this book, Weber's organizational and theoretical concept is applied to a contemporary issue, problem focus group behavior. The Typology defines, describes, and classifies various roles (think of these "characters") that are commonly played in focus groups and other small group settings.* These roles are given descriptive names such as Dominator and Wallflower. The types are defined by the behavior witnessed in focus groups during a 23-year career as a moderator and observer of group interaction. Feedback from professional moderators in workshops and informal review of earlier versions of the Typology have served to validate, confirm, and more carefully describe the types. The Typology is not all-inclusive, nor will any participant fit perfectly into any one type.

* Max Weber, a German sociologist and economist (1864–1920) developed the notion of the ideal type. It is an analytical construct that provides a basis for comparison, especially comparison of behavior. The ideal type involves accentua-tion of typical courses of conduct. Ideal type has nothing to do with morally correct, statistical averages or preferable behavior. Weber himself wrote: "An ideal type is formed by the one-sided accentuation of one or more points of view and by the synthesis of a great many diffuse, discrete, more or less present and occasionally absent concrete individual phenomena, which are arranged according to those one-sidedly emphasized viewpoints into a unified analytical construct."
See Coser (1977) for more complete, detailed, and formal definition of ideal type.

There have been several efforts to identify and classify various types of behavior in focus groups, but to date no one has proposed a complete typology. Goldman and McDonald provide a strong foundation for this current work in *The Group Depth Interview: Principles and Practice* (1987). They describe "destructive domination" by the "Intimidator" and the "Pontificator." Goldman and McDonald also describe and classify the "Passive Acquiescent" and the "Moderator's Ally."

Both Krueger (1987) and Mariampolski (2001) provide brief sections in their respective books on problem participant types. Krueger discusses four types: the "Expert," the "Dominant Talker," the "Shy Participant," and the "Rambler." Mariampolski refers to "Disruptive Respondents," "Latecomers," "Dominant Respondents," "Passive Respondents," "Compliant Respondents," "Liars," and "Rambling, Unfocused Respondents."

FIGURE 2.1A

Typology of Problem Participant Behavior

*Defining Characteristics of Four Types That Are **Always** Problems*

Characteristic Behavior

Dominator	Cynic	Hostile	Intoxicated
• Long responses	• Negative toward everything	• Immediate demands for corrective action	• Slurred speech
• Frequently the first to answer	• Closed mind and body language	• May share many qualities with Dominator	• Sleepy, agitated, extreme behaviors
• Speaks with tone of self-appointed expert	• Sees fault in everything and everyone	• Angry, combative demeanor	• Behavior manifestations are related to the type, nature, and amount of drug abused
• Dismisses other participants' opinions	• Seems to enjoy being argumentative and taking the negative view	• May become irrational and incomprehensible as anger over-whelms ability to communicate	
• Challenges moderator for control of the group dynamic			

Non-Verbal Cues

Dominator	Cynic	Hostile	Intoxicated
• Sits directly opposite the moderator	• Shares some cues with hostile, though less confrontational	• Extreme body language	• Smells of alcohol or marijuana
• Extreme body language	• Smirks or rolls eyes in response to others' comments	• Documents prepared	• Red eyes
• Deliberative gestures, like finger pointing or table pounding	• Often will grimace, smirk or show other signs of disagreement and often disrespect when others speak	• Irritated, complains	• Fidgety
		• Confrontational demeanor	• Other signs of drug use
		• Often will confront hostess or other front-line personnel	

FIGURE 2.1B

Typology of Problem Participant Behavior

Defining Characteristics of Six Types That Are **Sometimes** *Problems*

Characteristic Behavior

Wallflower	Follower	Co-Moderator
• Seeks to be invisible in the group • Will only speak when spoken to directly • Answers in very short, shy, non-committal manner	• Expresses no personal opinion, only supports opinions of others • Always agrees with others • Repeats others' opinions • Easily persuaded	• Asks questions of the group • Re-directs moderator probes • Re-phrases moderator questions to the group • Seeks to summarize and analyze others
Blatherer	**Proselytizer**	**Joker**
• Long, off-topic, nonsensical responses • Especially eager to please the moderator • May string words together that have no apparent meaning or relevance to the topic	• Dogmatically argues that his/her point of view is correct • Cannot recognize or accept that others hold opposing opinions • Seeks to persuade, or lacking this, disregard other valid viewpoints	• Cannot be serious for extended periods • Everything is humorous • Makes jokes, pranks, funny faces or gestures, often at inappropriate times and far too frequently for a productive group

Non-Verbal Cues

Wallflower	Follower	Co-Moderator
• Takes most out of the way, inconspicuous seat in the room • Refuses eye contact with moderator or other participants • May slink or slump in his/her chair	• Shy; shakes head in agreement while others talk • Waits to follow lead of others in all regards • Resists being the first to talk by looking away as moderator asks questions	• Sits adjacent to moderator • Seeks to be "friends" or especially supportive of other respondents
Blatherer	**Proselytizer**	**Joker**
• Speaks without making eye contact with moderator or other respondents • Excessive gestures • Unaware or unresponsive to non-verbal cues to talk less	• Speaks to others in the group, not the moderator, as he/she seeks to persuade • May be especially loud, with appearance of expert	• Seems to prefer message T-shirts and baseball caps • Will tip his/her hand by being humorous, playful in waiting area

All of the types defined by these scholars and practitioners are valid. This book comments on these types and includes them, although with some slight variation in names and refinement of their respective defining characteristics. In many cases, the names here and the names used by others are similar, but not identical. (See Figure 2.2 for a list of names used in this book and the "aliases" or those names used by others.) This Typology forms the basis for early identification, prevention, and management strategies that are presented in subsequent chapters.

FIGURE 2.2

Ten Problem Types of Behavior in Focus Groups
Names and Aliases

Dominator	Dominant Respondent,[2] Intimidator,[1] Dominant Talker,[3] Pontificator,[1] Know-it-all, Expert
Cynic	Antagonist[1]
Hostile	Angry
Intoxicated	Disruptive[2]
Wallflower	Passive,[2] Uninvolved,[1] Shy[3]
Follower	Passive Acquiescent,[1] Compliant[2]
Co-Moderator	Moderator's Ally[1]
Blatherer	Rambler,[3] Rambling Unfocused[2]
Proselytizer	Advocate, Fanatic, Truth Police, True Believer, Ideologue, Inquisitor[4]
Joker	Jokester, Prankster, Class Clown

1. Mariampolski uses these terms
2. Goldman and McDonald use these terms
3. Krueger uses these terms
4. Suggested alternatives from Balch and Doner

It is important to emphasize that it is not the participant who is the problem, but rather his or her behavior. Often the people who exhibit problem behavior also are among those with the most insight to contribute. Every participant (okay, nearly every participant) has constructive, meaningful ideas and thoughts to share with the group. It is the moderator's job to manage the counterproductive behavior so that the gold mine of participant ideas and thoughts can surface. Moderators must work harder and dig deeper with some participants than others. Through understanding the various types or roles that often are played by participants, moderators can be better prepared to facilitate group dynamics effectively. Some of the behaviors described occur in almost every group. The Dominator is a type that frequently emerges in focus groups. Other behaviors occur much less frequently but when they do, they are nearly always problematic (for example, Intoxicated participants). The various types of problem behavior also occur more or less frequently depending on the type of participant—physicians, teenagers, beer drinkers, for example—and the type of participant is often driven by product, service, or content category and associated discussion topic.

Context, group content, and many other factors matter and must be taken into account when deciding how to respond to problem behavior (more on this in Chapters 3, 4, and 5). In general, though, moderators must act to manage problem behavior, not ignore it in the hope that it will go away. From simple non-verbal communication, like avoiding eye contact, to much more direct approaches, like reinforcing the ground rules, each moderator must develop specific tactics to work with and bring out the best of each participant.

Ten Problem Types of Behavior Defined

The Dominator

The first and most discussed type of problem behavior is the Dominator. The Dominator is characterized by frequently being the first to respond to the moderator's questions, taking on the role of self-appointed expert on the topic, replying with long responses, and denying the validity of alternative points of view.

There are many variations and combinations of behaviors that can be seen as dominant. Certainly, some Dominators pontificate more, and others may be defined more by their frequent and loud verbalization. Still, the Dominator is generally easy to identify. Typically, he (less often, she) sits directly opposite the moderator. Extreme body language—leaning far into the table, or pushing back extremely far from the table—is also indicative of the Dominator. Look for exaggerated gesticulation or dismissive comments or body language in response to alternative points of view.

The Dominant participant's behavior is problematic when others in the group feel intimidated or stifled. When the moderator senses that the Dominant participant's behavior is stifling the opinions of other participants, it is incumbent on the moderator to take corrective action (more on this in Chapters 3, 4 and 5). Judy Langer (2001) summarizes the problems caused by Dominators this way:

> Dominating respondents are a focus group bugaboo—and one of the main objections to using focus groups in the first place. These are the people who know it all (or think they do), who invariably answer every question first, who make others remain quiet and, worst, sometimes succeed in swaying other respondents. They distort the research process, becoming an obstacle to ascertaining individual opinions and creating a false sense of consensus. Troublesome respondents are not just annoying to the moderator and the back room clients, they also bother the rest of the group.   (page 128)

Dominators often cite their own education, experience, or purported unique knowledge to appoint themselves as the expert in the room. In some cases, especially in medical or business focus group settings, the Dominator may in fact know more than the other participants. It is important for the moderator to figure out if the Dominator is a "natural group leader" or really a Dominant participant.

Mariampolski (2006) defines a key subtype of Dominator, the "Rabbi" (see the War Story, page 82), who is truly more knowledgeable than others in the group and does not intend to disrupt or derail the discussion. Yet "Rabbis" are deferred to out of respect for their unique status.

A natural group leader emerges in nearly every group, but the litmus test for a Dominator is when others in the group become hesitant or fearful of relaying their own opinions and defer to the Dominator. Sometimes participants may defer because of the Dominator's sheer belligerence. However, in other situations the Dominator may be benevolent, but as a matter of education, status, personal experience or some other factor may, in fact, be perceived as knowing more than others in the group. As a result, others defer to the Dominator.

More often the case, especially in consumer focus groups, is that Dominators know no more than anyone else, they just want everyone to think that they do. After moderating many groups and seeing the same behavior over and over, it is pretty obvious that Dominators want, need, and seek control. There are a variety of methods to prevent, manage, and even leverage the Dominator that are presented in Chapters 3, 4 and 5.

The Hostile Participant

Truly Hostile participants are never benign for the group and therefore always a problem for the moderator. Hostile people usually have a reason for their extreme anger. In focus group situations, usually one of three factors is the cause. First, Hostile participants typically have had a problem with a product or service related to the focus group content. Second, the problem may be a negative experience with the focus group recruitment process, parking, directions, or facility. Third, the person may simply be mad at the world and may bring this anger with him or her to the focus group. It is important for the moderator to understand the source of the hostility to determine the course of action and management. In all cases, the Hostile participant perceives the focus group as a platform for complaints and an outlet for anger. Often Hostile participants seek compensation, relief, or correction of the problem they have had via the focus group process.

Hostile participants provide clues to their combative attitude by coming to the focus groups prepared with notes, photographs, and other documentation of their problematic product or service experience. Typical signs of anger—flushed face, rude treatment of the focus group host, belligerent interaction with other participants—are often readily apparent within a minute or two of encountering the Hostile participant. The Hostile behavior can be perceived as antagonistic to other participants. In extreme cases, the Hostile participant can be frightening or potentially violent. Hostile participants sometimes become incomprehensible or appear irrational as their anger overtakes their ability to communicate.

The Cynic

Extreme Cynics are nearly always a problem in a focus group, as their behavior can dampen group enthusiasm as well as bias other participants. Cynics question everyone's sincerity, and often add a sneer or an eye-roll just to make sure everyone knows they are "not buying it."

The Cynic often shares some characteristics with the Dominator and sometimes the Hostile participant as well. Cynics want to be the first to speak. They seek to diminish the opinions of others. The Cynic sometimes comes off as angry at the world, like the Hostile participant. Cynics are different in that their primary motivation is to reject every concept, every idea, and diminish everyone else's opinion. They seem motivated by negativity and want to share that sentiment broadly, whereas the Dominator is motivated by a desire for control and to be seen as the authority. Hostile participants, on the other hand, want to get their anger off their chests, and often want compensation for the perceived wrongs that have been done to them.

It is important for a moderator to distinguish between a "group of

Cynics" and a set of stimuli (advertising ideas, for example) that are so bad that no one in the group can provide an honest, positive appraisal. Typically, Cynics will announce their presence by the negative words and smirks they use for almost any topic or stimuli shown. If it is a situation where all of the stimuli are unappealing and participants are just being honest and forthright, this typically will come through by the same behavior repeating itself in multiple groups. In these cases, it is not the Cynic that is a problem, but rather that the key products or concepts tested do not resonate with the group.

The Intoxicated Participant

Intoxicated participants are characterized as having their behavior modified by drugs or alcohol. The Intoxicated participant is known to nearly every moderator. Most frequently, alcohol is to blame for Intoxicated behavior, but it is not the only intoxicant that can cause problematic behavior. Cocaine, marijuana, and other illegal drugs can modify a participant's behavior to the point where it becomes a problem for the focus group moderator, the other participants, and the client. Some of the most problematic behavior with Intoxicated respondents, however, stems from prescription drug use.

Like the Hostile participant, the extremely Intoxicated participant is almost always a problem. Though the frequency of occurrence is low, it will vary by topic. Of course, there are exceptions in the public health arena where sometimes alcoholics or others with drug addictions are the desired participant profile. Yet people with these profiles are almost always best interviewed individually rather than in groups.

The Wallflower

The Wallflower seeks to disappear and be as unobtrusive as possible in the group setting. She (less often he) will never be the first to answer, will not volunteer responses, and interacts in a shy, non-communicative style. Silence is the Wallflower's calling card; lack of eye contact is her signature.

Including the Wallflower in the discussion and pulling the opinions and beliefs out of Wallflowers is often a challenge. As with some of the other types, there are subtypes of Wallflowers. In some cases, Wallflowers may be so quiet because they were incorrectly recruited and do not know enough about the product or concept under discussion to contribute meaningfully. In these cases, they choose not to contribute because of fear of embarrassment. In these cases, the moderator should politely excuse the Wallflower, pay her, and send her home, indicating clearly that it was "our mistake."

Most of the time the Wallflower may just be shy. The Wallflower is more often than not a benign distraction in the group. There are techniques and tools that can be used (see Chapter 5) to include the Wallflower in the discussion. In most cases they work, but if after many attempts they fall short, the Wallflower's lack of participation rarely biases the rest of the group. Still, failing to effectively include the Wallflower is a source of lost information for the client and a missed opportunity for the moderator.

The Follower

The Follower is characterized by agreeing with the opinions of everyone else in the group. Easily persuaded and allergic to even friendly disputes, Followers may constantly change their opinions to be in line with the outlook of others.

Be sensitive to Followers who constantly, and apparently indiscriminately, shake their heads in agreement with every response. Present a concept and the Follower is sure to like it; that is, unless others do not. The Follower seeks to be in the majority and resists voicing an opinion that appears to be in even the slightest way contradictory to the majority or the group leader. Always seeking middle ground and leaving room for changing their minds also characterizes extreme Followers.

The Follower is the Dominator's ally and is in a symbiotic relationship with the Dominator. When the Dominator sees that he can

persuade or intimidate other participants in the group, his behavior
is reinforced and he acquires the control desired. The Dominator
wants to shape the opinion of the group and the Follower is happy
to be swayed.

Followers are particularly problematic when there are multiple versions of them in the same group. The more Followers present in the
group, the more likely that the Dominator will be effective in his or
her intimidation tactics and limit the quality of the research.

On the other hand, if there is no strong Dominator in the group,
and only one Follower, the Follower can be a reasonably benign char-
acter. Like the Wallflower, a Follower whose true opinion fails to be
uncovered is missing information for the client and a lost opportunity for the moderator. Problems occur in analysis, especially when
client observers do not recognize that the Follower's comments are
based on the opinions of others, rather than relaying her own unique
perspective.

The Co-Moderator

The Co-Moderator is characterized by trying to help the moderator
with the questioning and moderation of the group. Typically the Co-
Moderator will re-phrase the moderator's questions, offer the group
"clarification" of the moderator's questions, pose new questions to the
group, and seek to encourage or discourage responses from particular respondents. Co-Moderators will also sometimes summarize the
comments of other respondents and offer their analysis of the meaning of the comments to the group as a whole.

The Co-Moderator typically sits immediately adjacent to the moderator. In extreme cases, the Co-Moderator may even attempt to take
the traditional moderator's chair at the end of the table as people are
initially seating themselves. Co-Moderators are often extraordinarily
outgoing, curious, and gregarious, sometimes even starting their questioning in the waiting area before the group formally begins.

The Co-Moderator's behavior becomes problematic when it steers the conversation away from the research objectives, undermines the "lead" role that the moderator seeks to play, and threatens to mislead the group with erroneous summaries and instant analysis. When the Co-Moderator diverts the group from achieving its research objectives, it is the moderator's responsibility to take corrective action (see Chapter 5).

Co-Moderators can indeed be the moderator's friend. If they are on the mark with probes and requests for clarification, they can help build a productive group interaction. The wise moderator can choose to allow Co-Moderators their role with no infringement on the role of the true moderator.

The Blatherer

The Blatherer is characterized by responding to the moderator's questions with long, often nonsensical responses. Blatherers are especially eager to please and seem to believe that the more words they use the more they will be liked by the moderator and the rest of the group. Blatherers are often so eager to please and to play the role as a talker that they will overdo it. Other variations include those who seem nervous to the point where they find it hard to respond meaningfully, so they string together series of words in incomprehensible ways.

Unlike some of the other problem types defined above, Blatherers do not provide immediate clues to their problem behavior by seat choice or other non-verbal cues. The Blatherer is all about verbalizing at length and without regard to the focus group content, the research objectives, or the ground rules. Others refer to this problem respondent type as a "Rambler" (Krueger 1988) or the "Rambling, unfocused" participant (Mariampolski 2001). As with some of the other types in this category, the Blatherer is a problem in a focus group setting based on how extreme the behavior is and how often it emerges in the focus group.

Mode of research—for example, the telephone focus group compared with a traditional in-person focus group—also affects the degree to which this type of behavior is a problem and the ease of controlling the behavior. During a telephone focus group, the moderator may choose to have the technician mute the Blatherer's connection. In a traditional face-to-face group, the moderator may need to use more subtle corrections and substantially more finesse to limit the amount of damage a Blatherer creates for the group dynamic and to allow enough time for the others to voice their opinions.

The Proselytizer

Dogmatically believing in his or her ideas to the exclusion of other points of view is a defining characteristic of the Proselytizer. Proselytizers are motivated by their allegiance, defending and promoting the product or service under discussion, or advocating for their unique point of view to the exclusion of all other opinions. While allegiance to the product or concept is a prerequisite for the Proselytizer, it is not enough to hold this strong opinion. Rather, the Proselytizer demands that all others believe as he or she does, or they are simply wrong.

In mild cases, Proselytizers may simply continue to defend or promote their ideas. In extreme examples, Proselytizers not only promote their own perspectives, but also seek to invalidate and diminish the opinions of others. It is this inability to allow any one else in the room to have an opposing opinion, recognized as valid, that makes the Proselytizer's behavior so problematic. Other participants in the session may hesitate to disagree with the strident Proselytizer. As a result, alternative opinions and free and open discussions are stifled or curtailed.

The Joker

As the name implies, the Joker is all about pranks, humor, laughs, and silliness. While teen and youth groups often include this type, there are many experiences and reports of adult Jokers. (See the War Story on page 105 about "Feel," the Joker). You will notice Jokers right away, as they are liable to crack a joke in the waiting room or within seconds of initially entering the focus group room.

Jokers become problems in the focus group when their jokes, or attempts at jokes, are offensive, disparaging, or attempt to take the group off subject for the sake of a few laughs. Jokers can become problematic when they choose to pick on a particular person (sometimes the moderator) in the room to be the butt of their jokes. Racially insensitive jokes, jokes laced with sexual innuendo or other off-color remarks made in attempts to get a laugh may make the rest of the participants uncomfortable and limit open, safe participation. Moderators must deal with this behavior or they are not delivering full benefit to the client.

Organizing the Problem Types

Figure 2.3 presents these ten types of problem behavior on a quadrant map. The two axes represent likelihood scales. The horizontal axis illustrates the likelihood that the problem types will attend or be present in the group. The vertical axis represents the likelihood that the problem type will act in a way that is problematic or hinders the group from achieving its objectives.

The upper-right quadrant (A) shows two problem participant types: the Dominator and the Cynic. These two problem types are very likely to appear in groups. The Cynic and the Dominator also are very likely to present problems to the moderator and hinder creating a safe, open, egalitarian environment for meaningful discussion. Nearly every group contains at least one person who seeks to lead the discussion, the Dominator. Similarly, one person often takes the role of the critic and in its extreme form, this becomes cynical and counterproductive. Moderator intervention is frequently required when these two types attend group discussion sessions.

The upper-left quadrant (B) shows two more problem types: the

Hostile and the Intoxicated. Though much depends on the group recruitment criteria, the nature of the group, and its objectives, these behaviors are rarely benign—and, thankfully, less likely to occur than Dominators and Cynics.

Hostile participants are more likely to appear in "customer satisfaction" groups, especially when the screening criteria seek those who have had unsatisfactory experiences with the client's product or service. This can be productive and informative for clients, but takes special attention from the moderator, as Hostile participants can be especially intimidating to others in the group. Intoxicated participants may appear in any type of group, but teen boys seem especially prone to coming to focus groups in altered states. Long multipart groups, especially common with mock jury trials, also provide an opportunity for drug-induced extreme behavior. In presenting these concepts and types in workshops, many moderators' have shared stories of mock jury trial participants coming back from the lunch break in altered mental states.

The lower-right quadrant (C) presents two more behavior types that appear in groups frequently, but are infrequently problems. These are the Wallflower and the Follower—"kissing cousins" in this Typology as they share some characteristics. The Wallflower seeks to disappear. Similarly, the Follower avoids even the mildest disagreement by concurring with all other comments, even those that are contradictory.

The lower-left quadrant (D) shows the three problem participant types—the Joker, the Proselytizer and the Blatherer—that occur less frequently and also are less frequently problems for the moderator and group. Again, depending on the type of group and nature of the objectives, the frequency of occurrence and the frequency of the behavior being problematic may vary. Extreme Blatherers, unrelenting Jokers, and excessively dogmatic Proselytizers occur less frequently and their behavior in the group setting is less often problematic than the Hostile or Intoxicated behavior presented in quadrant B. Still, these behaviors, when extreme, are never helpful and can create problems that require moderator intervention.

Finally, the Co-Moderator is placed exactly in the middle of both axes. This illustrates a third dimension, reflecting that the Co-Moderator may be an asset to the group. Recall that the Co-Moderator seeks to "assist" the moderator by asking questions of the group, re-directing moderator probes, and even summarizing and synthesizing the opinions of others. In some cases, Co-Moderators can become allies and when on-point, can give moderators a mental break, as they take on some of the responsibilities of the moderator.

FIGURE 2.3

Ten Problem Types Organized

Quadrant Map of Problem Participant Behavior Types

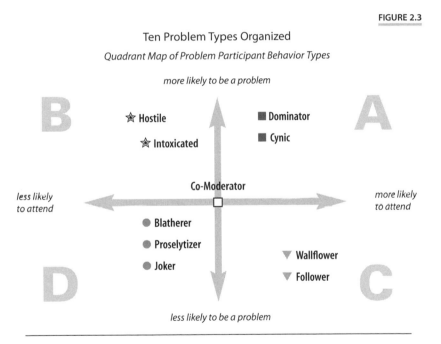

From a very practical perspective, this quadrant map illustrates that the new moderator should focus on understanding and learning to work with Dominators and Cynics, as they appear often and often cause problems with their behavior. Even experienced moderators should periodically check to make sure that they are managing these behaviors effectively in each group. Second priority should be given to learning to identify and manage the Intoxicated and the Hostile, as they nearly always require some form of moderator intervention. Less likely to occur and less likely to be a problem are the types presented in the lower half of the illustration.

Other Less Common Types

There are other types of problems that occur commonly in focus groups. The types described above are not mis-recruited participants. One of the pitfalls in focus group research is that there is sometimes miscommunication between the moderator and the field service recruiting the participants for the groups. Mistakes can occur. Other times, the pressure on the field service to deliver enough participants with certain characteristics leads to misrepresenting or modifying the characteristics of the participant. This becomes a problem when the participants appear in the group and innocently reveal that they do not meet the recruitment specifications. Still other times, the moderator may not have defined the recruitment specifications adequately, and this leads to participants with inappropriate characteristics.

Moderators can prevent some mis-recruitment problems by being reasonable with the recruitment specifications, clearly communicating with the recruitment firm, and personally re-screening the participants as they arrive at the focus group location and prior to inviting the participants into the group discussion room.

The problem types also exclude "Professional participants." As focus groups have become very common, and are not always operated by professionals with strict adherence to recruitment guidelines, the Professional participant has become more of a problem. The Professional participant is often a "cheater or repeater."*

* See the Market Research Association's **Newsletter** in February 2004 for an article entitled "A Practical Approach to Identifying Professional Focus Group Participants."

There are other problem types not addressed in the Typology that occur frequently enough to be described. These types almost always cause at least some irritation for the moderator and client observers, but rarely does their behavior become so problematic that the objectives of the group are compromised.

- *The Latecomer:* The Latecomer is a problem because the moderator seeks to complete a lot in short period of time. If a Latecomer is let into the group, a moderator must quickly re-state the basic ground rules and inform the Latecomer of the observers and video/audio recording. It is the moderator's responsibility to inform the facility representatives of how late, if at all, a tardy participant will be allowed into the group.

- *The Insider:* "I've done many focus groups." "I know the president of your client's company." "I used to be a focus group moderator in a former life." "I was a salesman for this product." "I am the original inventor of the product/service." Insiders can be a form of Dominator, where they seek authority by their insider status. Usually it is best to pay and send them home, quickly.

- *Whisperer/Sidebar Seeker:* These are participants who prefer to speak in whispers, and only to the participant sitting next to them. Simply asking the Sidebar Seeker to speak up and share with the group usually works to curtail this behavior.

- *The Flirt:* There are those who seek to flirt with the other participants and/or the moderator. It is surprising the large number of reports from moderators about participants "leering" at other participants. Similarly, there are more than a few stories from moderators who have been propositioned by participants following the group. Best bet is to politely ignore, and stay in group situations; if this does not work, turn the Flirt over to support personnel for payment and directions home.

- *Profane:* Profanity is dependent on context, but in some cases it can be out of place and inappropriate. Depending on the situation, a lighthearted "let's keep this conversation family style" might work to curb the profanity. Other times, if none of the participants appear bothered by the use of profane words, it may be best to simply show disapproval with body language, rather than a verbal correction.

• *Racist, Sexist Comments:* Racist and sexist comments in groups are particularly difficult to deal with. On one hand, the moderator may be insulted by the comments. Similarly, other participants may be insulted or at least made to feel uncomfortable by the derogatory comments. On the other hand, however, sexism, racism and other forms of discrimination may reveal specific insights about the group being studied. So the use of slurs may, in fact, be data for analysis. The general rule I suggest is that if the comments directly offend anyone in the group, the moderator should indicate that the language should not be used again. Similarly, if the moderator can determine that the offensive comments provide an impediment to meeting the research objectives, the offensive comments should be stopped. Offending solely the moderator's personal sensibilities is not enough reason to intervene.

• *Cell Phone/PDA Addicts:* Most facilities request that participants turn off their phones before entering the focus group room. Still, there are participants who cannot control their need to instant message, talk on their cell phones, or send messages via their PDAs. Including a comment in the introduction can help control cell phone addicts. In extreme cases, the moderator must ask the cell phone addict to step outside the focus group room if he or she must speak on the phone. If you sense or know you have a cell phone etiquette problem, here is a line you can use:

> *"I know that most if not all of you need to stay connected to work or home. But please, turn your cell phones to silent or vibrate, and if you must take an emergency call, please step outside and return to our group discussion as quickly as possible."*

- *Fidgeters:* These table-tappers, ice-crunchers, knuckle-crackers, and fingernail-chewers are more bothersome to some moderators and participants than others. If the behavior is extreme, the moderator can always ask the participant to recall that all of this is recorded, and "Who wants to listen to participants chewing ice for 120 minutes?"

- *Acutely Ill:* Respondents with coughs, colds, or flu pose another distraction. Once identified, it may be best to pay and send these participants home with sympathy.

- *Hearing/Speech Problems:* Every reasonable effort should be made to accommodate those with hearing or speech disabilities. Good recruiters can often identify these people beforehand and then decisions can be made as to how to accommodate their opinions. Balch and Mertens (1999) conducted research with hearing impaired participants of various types. Key findings from their research include:

  - Hearing impaired participants can be highly productive focus group participants; managing the physical environment (proximity of tables, chairs, participants and interpreters) is critical;

  - Moderators must be highly vigilant; more time is often needed than with a group with normal hearing;

  - Specific communication alternatives, like American Sign Language, Mexican Sign Language, or the use of hearing aids can assist the groups.

  - Moderators need to specifically understand the nature of the participants hearing (and/or speech) impairment so appropriate devices or support (interpreters) can be provided.

- *Uninvited Guests:* Participants who bring children, spouses, or others not specifically invited to the focus group facility can be sent home without provision of the incentive, assuming the para-

meters for participation are clearly stated in the screener and confirmation letters.

• *Language Limitations:* Those who do not speak the language used
in the focus group as their first language or have an accent that
is difficult to understand require the moderator to work harder.
Attempt to summarize and repeat the participant's comments and
then verify accuracy with both the participant with the accent as
well as others in the group. Sometimes clients request that participants with language limitations be excused, but be careful, as
they may constitute a substantial portion of the target audience
and have significant insight to offer.

• *Concealed Weapon Carriers:* There are reports of participants car-
rying concealed weapons into focus groups. It is legal in many
states to carry concealed weapons and unless the facility makes
a formal statement to all participants that this is not allowed, the
participant may be exercising his or her legal rights. Some moderators now explicitly request this policy in directions to the facility. If not, and a participant sees
another participant's weapon, it is judgment call
as to how to handle the situation. Typically, as
long as the Concealed Weapon Carrier appears
to have no malice intent, the formerly concealed
weapon is best ignored.*

* Alison Murphy in the August 2006 issue of QRCA's newsletter QRCA Connections describes her experiences with a concealed-weapon carrier in a focus group room.

• *Sympathy Seekers:* Occasionally, a participant will come to a
focus group and reveal so much, so quickly about his or her
problems and bad luck, that other participants in the group
are made uncomfortable and the discussion may become side-
tracked. Empathize with the Sympathy Seeker quickly, and then
move on. Something like, "I am sure we are all sorry for your
difficult situation, and many of us also have had difficult times.
But tonight let's focus on the issue at hand, not your set of personal concerns."

FIGURE 2.4

Ten Problem Types of Behavior in Focus Groups
Nutshell Summary

Dominator	Seeks to take control of the group, diminish others' opinions
Cynic	Rejects every concept, idea and is negative toward everything and everyone
Hostile	Angry, combative demeanor, often seeks corrective action
Intoxicated	Behavior is dramatically modified through the use of alcohol or other drugs
Wallflower	Shy, non-communicative, non-responsive, seeks to disappear
Follower	Easily and frequently influenced by the opinions of others
Co-Moderator	Seeks to assist the moderator by asking questions of the group and re-directing moderator probes, sometimes acts as instant analyst summarizing the meaning of others' comments
Blatherer	Speaks far too long and far too often; comments are incomprehensible or far off-topic
Proselytizer	Dogmatically argues that his/her point of view is correct and seeks to persuade or invalidate others' preferences/opinions
Joker	Every word or action of others is a signal to make fun, to pull a prank, or seek to be humorous, often so that he or she may bring attention to himself/herself

Summary

In this chapter, the Typology of ten problem behaviors in focus groups has been presented. With a clear understanding of the types of problem behavior a moderator may encounter, the moderator will be more likely to recognize the behavior quickly and be armed to prevent the problem behavior, effectively manage it, or avoid it altogether. Not all behaviors are always problematic. Four behavior types including the Dominator and the Cynic are almost always problems. These types also frequently attend focus groups. The Hostile and Intoxicated participants attend less frequently than the Dominator and the Cynic, yet their behavior is also almost always problematic.

Five types of participant behaviors are sometimes, but not always, problems for the moderator and the client. These are the Follower, Wallflower, Blather, Proselytizer, and Joker. Depending on how extreme their behavior is and the context, these behaviors may or may not be benign. The Co-Moderator can be a problem sometimes, but also may be helpful to the group. For this reason, the Co-Moderator is positioned at the intersection of the lines on the quadrant map (Figure 2.3) where this organizational approach is summarized.

Tough Guys Gone Wild

Kristin Schwitzer
Beacon Research, Severna Park, MD

I ALWAYS ENJOY the opportunity to moderate a group of respondents who are not at all like me. I welcome the chance to see into another world, as it stretches me both personally and professionally.

On one such project, I was working with a bunch of blue-collar workers from the construction industry: general contractors, plumbers, fence builders, deck builders, and even excavators (the guys who dig the holes in the dirt in the first place so other guys can build something). Without exception, these men had never participated in a focus group before, were not accustomed to being in an office, and typically did not spend two consecutive hours talking instead of working with their hands, let alone talking with a woman. As a female qualitative research consultant, I was definitely getting a group of respondents who were not at all like me. I was in for an experience that would test my on-the-spot thinking!

Before long, I had these guys talking plenty, though they were very loud and a tad unruly. As I always do in my guidelines at the beginning of a group, I had asked them to *please speak one at a time* so that we could hear one another, and so that I could actually hear their comments when later listening to the tape of our discussion. That guideline was quickly forgotten and I had to repeatedly interject to keep control of the group. Occasionally, I would use a hand gesture and eye contact with my verbal correction: I would put my arm out straight in the direction of the inter-rupter with a flat hand in the recognizable "stop" position. Sometimes I would use my physical presence to regain control by getting up out of my chair and standing right behind the person who had interrupted. Keeping eye contact with the person who had been trying to talk first encouraged that person to keep going and, when I broke eye contact with the inter-rupter, the interrupter soon stopped talking. About an hour into the ses-sion, I felt we were making fairly good progress on learning whether my client's current marketing efforts were reaching this target and effectively communicating with them. Everyone was contributing, and I felt I was get-ting what my client needed.

I launched the next topic and the group suddenly took off. I had hit a *hot button*. They all had a strong opinion on this one, and all wanted to share it at the exact same time. Each tried talking louder than the next. My voice could not even be heard in the ruckus and, even though I was the only person standing, I could not get the group's attention. I knew I had to try something more drastic, and quickly. It was clear I had lost control.

Thinking back to the respondents' self-introductions, it was obvious I had a group of sports fanatics: football, basketball, baseball, you name it. Watching sports was how they spent most of their free time. I abruptly put my hands into a "T" (an athlete's sign for "time out") and physically leaned over the table as far as I could, all with a smile on my face and a twinkle in my eye . . . and not a word. The guys broke into laughter and immedi-ately stopped talking, giving me the floor again. I'd never tried this before (nor since), but it definitely worked to give me back control of my group and make the second half equally productive.

Lessons Learned

1. Be willing to take a risk and try something new if your tool box of tricks is not working.

2. Personalize your solution to your audience; try to relate it to what's important to them.

3. A smile can you give you a bit of liberty when trying a more abrupt solution.

4. Act quickly, should you lose control of your group.

5. Make sure your upfront guidelines include the *speak one at a time* point so that you have permission to interject later, if needed.

6. Recognize that your respondents have valuable opinions to share even though their behavior may not be ideal.

A Tale of Two Truth Cops

Proselytizer #1

George I. Balch, PhD

Balch Associates, Oak Park, IL

IN 1992, I was crossing the country doing focus groups to refine the communication strategy for the National Cancer Institute's "5 A Day for Better Health" media campaign. The campaign had started without any consumer-based research and I was hired to explore links and gaps between wanting to eat more fruits and vegetables (which a large and growing segment of adults did) and actually doing it. Nutrition, health and eating—what a great assignment! The research design I developed called for "template groups" in which one group of "doers," those who already ate five or more servings of fruits and vegetables daily, was observed by another like them in all respects except that they did not eat their five servings daily ("non-doers"). This meant we had other focus group participants, as well as clients, in the back room. The audience outnumbered the participants.

In the first group, in Philadelphia, all was going well as the participants, women with children, started introducing themselves and how fruits and vegetables fit into their families' lives. They quickly warmed up and started sharing stories, until one woman, hearing a story about how another young mother was feeding her baby milk, jumped in and chastised the mother for feeding her child fat. Fat, she said, was poison. It would build up in her child's blood vessels and cause an early heart attack, just as it did with her father. The mother was taken aback, both by the story and by the teller's certainty and barely controlled rage.

A couple of other participants gingerly disagreed—everyone needs some fat in their diets; babies need milk; and so forth, all in calming ways. The attacking woman would not listen; she knew that fat was poison. A bit later she attacked another mother's feeding habits in much the same way. Nobody responded to her. And that was about the last of what she had to say for the session.

When the women in the back room—the non-doers—convened, they expressed concern about "fanatics" who wanted to tell them how to eat and feed their families. They kept talking about it through much of their session. They found it off-putting and not persuasive. We had discovered a "not-so-hot" button.

Proselytizer #2

George I. Balch, PhD & Lynne Doner, MA
Lynne Doner Consulting, Arlington, VA

IN 2004, we were conducting computer-assisted, telephone focus groups about social support for children for a non-profit organization that works to prevent child abuse. Participants were parents who were interested in the wellbeing of children. They came from a range of big cities such as New York, to small towns in California and everything in between, culturally speaking.

One group had a participant from a small Texas town who kept commenting sarcastically and critically on the problems that some people identified as the result of where they live (in urban centers, two of them in New York City). She went so far as to say, in a scolding tone, "How can you live there?" When we turned to identifying the kinds of social resources that address those problems, she promptly declared that every community has the only organization it needs. It was, of course, their church, she said. Participants had various comments on that assertion, all of them couched in direct, but polite language: what if someone is not Christian; our church is in trouble right now; we don't belong to a church. The participant from Texas would not leave it alone; she made a snide remark about the Catholic Church and another about New York City.

Just as we were ready to have the telephone operator pull the Texas participant off the line, thank her, pay her the incentive, and tell her she was done, the moderator reminded the group that there was a lot to cover, so it was important to stay on the topic. The participant from Texas then disappeared from our computer screen; she had hung up.

Lessons Learned

1. The Proselytizer and how people react to her or him can be very important in developing campaigns. In Philadelphia, a little bit of proselytizing went a long way in turning off the non-doers. That insight and additional corroborating data proved helpful in formulating the campaign.

2. The Proselytizer in the Philadelphia group may have given some of the others in the group ungrounded fears about how they were feeding their families, and as a result, I have adopted the practice of ending a group by dispelling any inaccurate, risky information that has been passed along in the group conversation. When possible, I try to have an expert on the topic as an observer and have her or him come out and provide that information. At the very least, I try to provide a pamphlet or something with the latest consumer-friendly scientific information. When you deal with health issues people can be hurt by misinformation. Doubtless that is true of some other issues, too.

3. When a person has strong views that he or she persistently tries to impose on others in a focus group, the group may handle it in different ways, such as:

    a. uniting against the person directly;

    b. trying to minimize the person's intrusion by ignoring him or her once they recognize the problem (as with Proselytizer #1); or

    c. waiting for the moderator to intervene.

4. Lynne and I have found it wise to let the group try to manage itself first. Their efforts to do so sometimes stimulate considerable energy and openness. And shutting someone down early may intimidate some group members.

5. Other times, especially if the Proselytizer is insistently argumentative or verbally abusive and unresponsive to social cues, the moderator may need to remind all of the participants of the purpose of the session—to express opinions about the topic at hand in the limited time we have. That is what Lynne did. From the Texan's sudden departure it seems that she had come to the group for a different purpose.

6. If a clear reminder about the purpose of the group doesn't get the Proselytizer on track, it may be necessary to get her or him to leave. There are several ways to do this:

    a. On the telephone the operator (prepared in advance for such a situation and triggered by the moderator when it arises) can take the disruptive participant off the conference line and politely acknowledge his or her contributions, for which the incentive will be paid as promised. All of this happens quickly and out of earshot, while the group continues.

    b. Computer-assisted telephone conferencing makes it even easier, by allowing unobserved direct contact among moderator, operator, and observer as to when and how to do this. For example, while the group was in progress—say, while a participant was speaking—the moderator could have asked the operator to remove Proselytizer #2.

7. Face-to-face focus groups may require something like a note sent to

the back room or to the facility to notify the disruptive participant that he or she has a phone call and must come with his or her coat right away.

8. It is the moderator's job to run the group and keep it on track, even if he or she vehemently opposes or feels offended by a participant's opinion. That kind of respect for both the group task and the participants' rights to their opinions can do much to help the group be productive and feel involved and valued.

CHAPTER 3

Early Identification of Problem Behavior

━━━━━━━━━━ *In the previous chapter,* ten common problem types of behavior are described and categorized. Depending on the product or service category and associated participant types, some problem types may be encountered more or less frequently than others. Yet one of the most difficult challenges for a moderator is to recognize the problems early enough in the process so that prevention tactics can be implemented (described in Chapter 4). If we fail to prevent the problem behavior, management tactics can be used (described in Chapter 5), but prevention is best. The key to prevention is early identification—the focus of this chapter.

Developing the descriptions and reflecting on the "War Stories" about the problem types is not just an enjoyable exercise. It allows us to categorize people by the behavior they exhibit so we have some structure for potential intervention and problem behavior correction. It also allows us to reflect on the experiences we have had with each of the problem types and also on the methods we use (or do not use) to prevent and effectively manage the behavior. Sometimes, in hindsight, the behavior is even funny, or at least entertaining. Many times we wish we had acted a little differently in order to produce a different outcome.

Creation of the Typology is anything but an academic exercise. The Typology has been developed for the specific purpose of being used as a tool for moderators to recognize the signs of problem behavior early in the process. Early identification is one of the three key strategies for actively and effectively dealing with the inevitable problems that occur in focus groups. Beyond knowing the types, the moderator should assess the participant pool prior to, and early on, in each group session. Critical to early identification is being sensitive to the many little cues and clues that are observable about participant behavior. This will allow the moderator to be pro-active in managing the problem.

Know the Types

Becoming aware of the problem behavior and being sensitive to it is the first step in preventing and managing it. Basic awareness of the problem types coupled with the realization that some type of problem behavior is going to be present in nearly every group is critical for every moderator. Seasoned moderators develop this heightened awareness and sensitivity with experience and trial and error. Some call it "moderator's intuition." Less experienced moderators can move down the path of effectively addressing problem behavior more quickly if they know the types. As this book was in development, some colleagues reported carrying earlier drafts of the Typology with them as they traveled to groups to enhance their own awareness and sensitivity.

Perhaps some moderators fail to identify problem behavior early in a group because of all of the other challenges they encounter. From interacting with clients on everything from content to stimulus, to travel logistics, to focusing on the guide and the objectives it is designed to achieve, the focus group moderator must be able to multitask. The broad range of things a moderator must manage, especially at the beginning of each group, is extensive, but it should be a priority to identify potential problem behavior.

FIGURE 3.1

Clues and Cues to Help Identify the Problem Types

*Four Types That Are **Always** Problems*

Dominator	Cynic	Hostile	Intoxicated

• First to answer
 	
• Sits directly opposite moderator
 	
• Folded arms, closed stance
 	
• Loud, long answers
 	
• Challenges moderator for control of group
	• Displays negative behavior by deriding others' ideas
	
	• Folded arms, closed stance
	
	• Often will sit opposite the moderator, similar to Dominator
	
	• Often offers early complaint about discussion process
		• Has materials, documentation, photos, letters prepared
		
		• Seeks corrective action
		
		• May reveal himself to hostess or other front-line personnel
			• Smells of alcohol or marijuana
			
			• Depending on drug being used, may be:
			  • *Fidgety*
			  • *Anxious*
			  • *Sleepy*
			  • *Incoherent*

*Six Types That Are **Sometimes** Problems*

Wallflower	Follower	Co-Moderator
• Seeks to be inconspicuous by sitting away from moderator • Never volunteers • Speaks only when spoken to, and then, in a very soft voice, with abbreviated comments	• Nods head frequently • Will wait for others to answer before speaking • Rarely volunteers	• Sits next to moderator, on direct right or left • May begin asking questions in waiting area or before the group actually starts • Addresses group with eye contact rather than speaking with moderator

Blatherer	Proselytizer	Joker
• Speaks without making eye contact • Oblivious to gentle and non-verbal cues to shorten comments • Takes far too long introducing himself/herself	• Acts easily offended by others with a differing view • Speaks directly to other participants in effort to persuade	• Favors message T-shirts, baseball caps • Will reveal himself quickly by making jokes early in discussion, usually during introductions

Screening and Recruitment

Many pre-group activities can influence the type and amount of problem behavior a moderator may encounter. These include:

- Acquisition of the list or source for sampling;

- Design and content of the screening instrument;

- Attitude and communication style of the recruiter;

- Professionalism and tone of the follow-up and confirmation letters or calls, and;

- Nature and value of the incentive.

These pre-group factors can influence both identifying potential problems early in the process and then taking steps to prevent the problem behavior.

List and Sample Acquisition

Moderators should know, for every group, the source and characteristics of the sample. Answer these basic questions:

- Were participants recruited from a facility's or recruiters' database? If so, what can you learn about the participants from the database information? How was the potential focus group participant database created?

- Were participants recruited from a client's customer base, lost customer, prospect, or some other client-produced list? If so, what criteria were used to select potential focus group participants? How was the list created?

- If a list was purchased, what criteria were used to select the potential participants? What is known about the list's source?

- Was the sample created in such a way that participants may self-select themselves into the group, as in bulletin board or mass email recruits?

The moderator should take steps to know all of these factors well before the first recruitment call is made because the sample source can have a significant impact on the frequency and type of problem behavior the moderator encounters.

For example, if the sample was selected using respondents to a clients' customer satisfaction survey, and only those who report satisfaction on the low-end of the quantitative scale are recruited, the moderator should be ready for a higher percentage of Hostile and Cynical participants. Similarly, be especially cautious of facility database recruits who are more likely to be Co-Moderators or Followers if they have too much prior focus group experience.

Self-selected samples are perhaps the most unpredictable for the moderator. Ads placed in local papers, notices placed on electronic bulletin boards (e.g., *craigslist*), or mass emails to vaguely defined groups of prospective participants all have the potential for participants to "self-select" into the group. While these techniques may be necessary to locate low-incidence populations or may be implemented to save money on the recruitment, they also may have an effect on the type of participants in the room during the group and the types of problem behaviors they exhibit. Knowledge, awareness, and sensitivity to the sample source are the first of many clues a moderator can use to help identify problem participant behavior early.

Screeners and Recruiters

Perhaps the best way to identify problem participants is with the help of carefully designed screeners applied by well-trained, well-educated, experienced recruiters. After the sample source has been identified, the screener and the people who use it (recruiters) are two critical factors.

Screeners

Writing effective screeners is an art form too complex to address completely in this book. There are some good resources for writing great

* See "You Get What You Ask For,"
prepared by Merrill Shugoll and
other members of the MRA/QRCA
Screener & Rescreener Task Force.
Commissioned by the MRA/QRCA
Joint Committee Fall 1999.

screeners.* Survey design training and experience can be very helpful in designing effective screeners. Clear definition of recruitment specifications and agreement among the client, the moderator, and recruitment firm about the feasibility of the recruit is also essential. Still, a few comments are in order about screeners and how they can be used in combination with professional recruiters to identify potential problem behavior early in the process.

First, the single most important word any screener writer (often times the moderator, but not always) can use on the screener to be sent to a recruiter is "DRAFT." Chosen carefully, professional recruiters can assist researchers in writing and implementing effective screeners. I suggest listening carefully to critiques or concerns expressed by the recruiters as perhaps the most important step a moderator can take to ensure effective recruitment.

Apart from writing questions that carefully identify the participant characteristics, making a courteous request for opinions from the recruiter can help set the appropriate tone for the eventual group discussion.

A carefully worded invitation script (example below) also can prevent a lot of minor problems in a focus group. For example, participants bringing children or others with them to the facility or focus group site, participants arriving late (even a little can cause problems), and participants forgetting their reading glasses are easily preventable problems.

Recruiters

Most commonly, focus group participants for traditional face-to-face groups and telephone groups are recruited by the hosting focus group facility, typically by phone, but increasingly by email. Online groups are more often recruited by email. The profession of qualitative research has evolved in somewhat odd ways. Field facilities often provide both hosting and recruiting services. Yet the skill-set and type of personnel needed to effectively and professionally recruit participants for focus groups is far different from the skills, knowledge, and disposition needed to be an able and effective host.

Moderators can benefit from developing long-term relationships with professional recruiters, both locally and nationally. In some instances, this may mean recruiting from outside the geographic area where the groups will be held. There are trade-offs. Local recruiters usually have the same accents as the potential participants and know the local geography ("the facility sits behind the courthouse") so they can direct the participant to the location. But using local recruiters also means that the moderator is interacting with different recruiters each week and for each project. This prevents the type of open, collegial sharing of information that comes from building a long-term relationship with professional recruitment firms.

While many of the chains of focus group facilities offer recruitment across many markets, still the connection to the specific recruiter is critical.

My personal preference is to use a national recruiting firm (with recruiters located in many major markets across the states). This allows for time to develop trusting relationships with the individual recruiters, as well as the recruiting supervisor. This trust allows them to share concerns about the screener or alert me to potential participant behavior problems that may occur during the upcoming groups.

Most importantly, detailed information from the recruiters that helps identify any potential problem behavior in an upcoming group will likely be shared openly. "Sarah, the woman I recruited for group 1, seems really upset" (potential Hostile). "Mrs. W., recruited for group 2, went on and on when we talked on the phone. I had to cut her off" (potential Blatherer). "Joe S., seemed to want to know everything about the group, the client, the product, the facility, etc. He started asking me more questions than I asked him" (potential Dominator or Co-Moderator). Without a trusting, collegial relationship with a recruiting firm, it is unlikely that the moderator will be made aware of these potential problems.

The key to working effectively with recruiters is to go beyond the recruiting supervisor and talk directly with the people that have contact with the potential participants on the phone or via other recruitment methods (mall or store intercepts, for example). Much of the information that can be derived from screening stems from nuance, the tone of voice the potential participant uses, and other factors that will not come through in a structured screening instrument. Supervisors see the tallies, the call records, and are ultimately concerned with "filling the group."

The actual interviewers or recruiters on the phone have direct contact with the potential participants. This allows them to report hunches or feelings about possible problems. Working together with a trusted, professional, and experienced recruiting organization, whether internal or external to the facility, can help identify and prevent problem behavior in focus groups.

Incentives

Cash (or check) incentives are common. But incentives that are too high may attract participants who are attending only to receive the incentive. Other types of incentives such as "see the newest technology" or "meet with the engineers" may have a different type of draw. The moderator needs to carefully consider the appeal of the incentive used and how it may affect the behavior in the group.

One key category familiar from two decades of work with automotive companies provokes another set of concerns. Many times "car buffs" are attracted to focus groups because they believe (sometimes incorrectly) that they will have the opportunity to complain about some specific feature or function of a vehicle. Others want to suggest an idea for a new product concept. When they become aware that the focus of the group is specific and different from the purposely vague invitation, they can sometimes become disenchanted and exhibit problem behavior in the groups. When setting incentives, be reasonable. To do this, talk to local experts in the area where you will be conducting the research to get a sense of local norms and customs. Try to set incentives so that they are neither so high as to draw only those who want the money, or too low, so that the recruitment becomes impossible. If you are using non-monetary incentives or some combination, be especially mindful of the effect that incentives can have on the composition of the group.

Invitation Scripts and Method

There are many different ways to invite people to a focus group. Below is an example invitation script designed to prevent some common problems.

Sample Focus Group Invitation

On behalf of (SPONSOR or RESEARCH FACILITY), we would like to invite you to participate in a research study to be conducted in (LOCATION). This will be an evening meeting that will last no longer than two hours. Parking is free and easily accessible.

You will be compensated ($XXX CASH OR CHECK) for your participation. In addition, we will be serving (A LIGHT SNACK/DINNER). Our group discussion will take place on (DAY OF WEEK), (DATE) at (TIME). You will be in a group with other consumers like yourself, talking about (SUBJECT MATTER). Please be assured that this is strictly a research study and there will be no sales pitch.

Q: May I schedule your participation?

    a. *No* (THANK AND TERMINATE)

    b. *Yes* (CONTINUE)

At this time, I would like to verify your address and other information.

Recruiter completes contact information below:

NAME
_____

ADDRESS
_____

CITY
_____

STATE _____ ZIP _____

PHONE DAY
_____

PHONE EVENING
_____

EMAIL
_____

AGE _____ GENDER _____

INTERVIEWER'S NAME
_____

Thank you very much for your willingness to participate in this focus group discussion. In the past, our guests have found the experience to be both informative and enjoyable. We are confident you will too.

I just have a few last things to tell you before we finish.

Please plan to arrive at the facility at least 15 to 30 minutes before the session starts. The discussion will start promptly at (TIME) p.m. and late arrivals will not be allowed into the discussion. Please bring reading glasses if you wear them. This group has been very specially selected, so please do not send a substitute. Also, because we cannot accommodate extra visitors, please do not bring friends, relatives, or children with you. The invitation to the group is for you only.

Finally, we will call you the day before your appointment to remind you of the time and date. In the meantime, if you have any questions—or should you need to reschedule or cancel your appointment time—please call (NAME) at (AREA CODE/NUMBER) anytime between 9 a.m. and 5 p.m.

A letter will be sent via e-mail or mail to confirm the discussion times and provide participant instructions in writing, including the exact location and directions. Thank you, again, for your cooperation. We look forward to your participation!

Follow-up Scripts and Confirmation Methods

There are many ways to write effective confirmation letters. From experience, here are some items to include in your confirmation letters to prevent problems:

- Return address;
- Map and clear directions to the facility (if it is be conducted in-person);
- Phone number to follow-up;
- Reminder about reading glasses (if appropriate);
- Reminder about no children, others (if appropriate);
- Appreciation for the participant's time;
- Emphasis that the groups are typically enjoyable and informative.

A confirmation phone call the day before the group also can serve to improve show-up rates and help the moderator become aware of any last minute cancellations or other problems.

On-Site: Greet, Meet, and Re-screening

A significant step that moderators can take to identify problem behavior early in the process is to greet and meet participants in the waiting area. The moderator can then begin to establish rapport, roles, and see if there are any problems readily apparent with the participants.

This is not feasible in every situation. In many cases, the moderator may be preparing for the next group, debriefing with clients, or attending to a range of other tasks. Sometimes the physical arrangement of the focus group location makes meeting and greeting folks less than ideal, especially when in hotel or conference room situations as there is no private place to speak with participants individually. Still, when feasible, the moderator can use the meet and greet in the waiting area to get a "feel" for the participants.

Using a re-screener is another way to identify problems early, as well as avoid the possibility that incorrectly recruited participants will enter the room and cause the moderator the embarrassment and disruption of needing to excuse a participant once the group starts. A re-screener is a brief questionnaire administered on site by an interviewer or is self-administered. It is usually a sub-set of questions from the screener asked during the recruitment process. Critical screening variables (use of client's product or service, for example) can be re-asked, sometimes with slightly different wording, to help ensure that the potential participant actually does qualify for the group.

When feasible, the moderator should act as the interviewer. This allows for one-on-one interaction prior to the group, between moderator and participant. Beyond the answers to the questions, the moderator can gather clues about any potential problem behavior. Most importantly, the moderator can use the re-screening process to begin to develop rapport and trust with the participants so that the discussion is more open and safe once the group begins.

If it is not practical for the moderator to play the role of the re-screener, there are alternatives.

Consider having the host or hostess re-screen or check the re-screeners. Then the moderator can consult with the hostess for alerts to any potential problems or inconsistencies. Another alternative, if the moderator is fortunate enough to be working with a colleague, note-taker, or other valued and insightful partner, is to ask the colleague to play this re-screener role. Finally, even if the moderator cannot re-screen, it is almost always possible to visit the waiting area, introduce him or herself, and ask some questions that will provide clues to problem behavior. For example:

- *How is everyone doing?* Note who speaks first, as this may be a clue to the potential Dominator. Note, also, if anyone has a long-winded, horribly convoluted answer. This may be a clue to a Blatherer. Be sensitive to how many ask the moderator questions: How did you get my name? Why are we here? Who are you? Who do you work for? These can all be clues to potential Cynics, Dominators, and Co-Moderators.

- *Did anyone have trouble finding the facility tonight?* Listen for complaints and maybe some underlying hostility.

- *How were the folks that called you on the phone? Were they polite and professional, or not?* Listen for complaints—their tone as well as their content.

Keen Observation

Pay close attention to how participants enter the room and where people sit. The first few minutes of a focus group are critical. The manner in which each participant enters the room, the chairs they sit in, and their body language in relation to other participants are all clues to the types of behavior you will encounter in that group.

Be aware of the participant who decides to sit directly across from the moderator. Be especially attentive if this is the first person to enter the room and also the first person to speak when asked an open-ended question of the entire group. None of these alone is a sure sign of a Dominator, but put them all together, add a bit of dismissive tone to his or her language, and the moderator is likely looking at a person whose behavior may become dominating.

Summary

There are several ways that a moderator can identify the potential for problem behavior before it occurs in the group. This includes careful and complete understanding of the sample source, working closely with recruiters, writing effective screeners, and being a keen observer of the behavior in the waiting room and the first several minutes of the group. Through being sensitive to all of these factors, moderators can identify potential problems early so they can prevent them.

The Dominant Kid

Jean McDonnell
JMD Research & Consulting, Chicago, IL

IT WAS JANUARY 1999, about a year and a half after I opened up shop as an independent qualitative researcher, and eight or nine years after I had earned my reputation in the industry as a "kids" research specialist. By this point in my career, I thought I had seen just about all there was to see in terms of "bad" behavior—from both sides of the two-way mirror. Truth is, in this particular case, I was more concerned with the clients in the back room than on anticipating potential problems with my next group of participants. This was a relatively large and important project to my clients and their agency. We were halfway through the project, the goal of which was to elicit children's responses to several new communication platform ideas. Unfortunately, none of the concepts shown in the first market had been well received by the kids. Despite some rushed attempts at revising the concepts, I was concerned that the changes had not gone far enough to make a real difference. And so I walked into the front room with my mind mostly in the back.

My groups that day started with 11- and 12-year-old boys, a gender and age group that (next to teens) has the dubious reputation for being one of the most difficult groups of respondents to facilitate. Ironically, the qualities that make this group so intimidating to many moderators are what I admire most about them. On the downside, these age groups of boys (typically 5th and 6th graders) have the potential to be silly, smart-alecky, goofy, impatient, easily bored, and candid to the point of being mean. Additionally, without guidance, they're apt to form and adhere to "leader-follower" group dynamics quite quickly. On the positive side, when their wild energy is properly channeled, these boys also are fun and funny, quick, engaging, smart, imaginative, realistic, and brutally honest.

In hindsight, my first mistake that day was in not paying enough attention to the needs of the kids initially and not properly channeling the energy of the room. I began the group in my usual manner with this age group: attempting to show "unconditional positive regard" for them and their opinions, encouraging group ownership and diversity of opinions, and setting the guidelines for acceptable behavior. Although I went through all the steps, I must not have had my heart (or head) in it, because it wasn't long before I began to lose control of this group. A Dominator quickly emerged who challenged my leadership and control of the group in a very aggressive manner. He was sly and subtle at first, doing his best at "pretending" to express genuine opinions, all the while working at getting the other kids to imitate his mock sincerity. The others were a little hesitant at first as to whom they would recognize as "leader." I was the adult, which meant I had instant authority, but Jeremy was clearly having more fun. One by one I saw the other kids being swayed over to join his "camp." I knew for sure that I was losing them when the worst concept of the bunch was revealed. In response to this concept—one which all kids in the previous groups had seen as "trite" and rejected hands down—Jeremy made a big show over how much he really "loved" this idea, making all the kids crack up over the obvious ridicule he was perpetrating.

I knew it was now or never and I had to make my move. I also knew I had two choices: either to get rid of this kid, and suffer a potential shut-down from the rest of the group in response to losing their leader, or to try to take back control of the group in a way that both the Dominator and Followers could respect. I knew the latter was the better choice but I wasn't sure how I was going to pull it off. My first thought was to remind the group of the guidelines they had agreed to at the beginning. I said something like: "I'm sensing that some of you aren't being totally honest with me about your opinions. Remember that you all agreed earlier to give us your honest opinions . . . " I stopped, knowing this tactic wasn't getting me anywhere. Then it hit me. I knew what to do.

Jeremy was dressed in the typical fashion of the day: baggy pants, expensive brand-label sneakers, long oversized T-shirt, and a baseball cap pulled snugly and long over his face. I suddenly realized that throughout the whole group I had trouble really seeing him, his cap covered so much of his face. So I amended my speech: "Oh yeah, and I want to remind you guys of another rule in here that I forgot to tell you about earlier. No baseball caps." With that, I walked up, gently yanked off Jeremy's cap, and placed it on the table next to him. Although my instincts were good, I wasn't prepared for the dramatic effect that this small action had on all of us.

Jeremy instantly froze. He became very quiet and withdrawn. It was obvious to see that he was embarrassed and felt "exposed"—both literally and figuratively. The rest of the group just looked at the two of us to see what would happen next. I tried to act as if nothing had happened and continued to ask for honest opinions in reaction to the concept. One by one the kids started telling me what they really thought, which was mostly negative but in a thoughtful, constructive way. Jeremy finally spoke up, very respectfully this time, and agreed with the others. He said he was "only kidding" when he said he liked it. As he went on to tell me how he really felt, with real sincerity, I knew that the power struggle for control of the group was over.

Lesson Learned

The lesson I learned in this situation was a big one. I learned not to "fight" for control, for to do so, there would have to be a loser, and thus everyone would lose. The objective is to find a way to even out the playing field, to rebalance the energy when it's gotten off kilter, but to do so in a way that allows the Dominator to back down respectfully. Although I've continued to issue a "no hat" policy in my groups with boys and men (and it works very well at helping to "open" guys up for honest conversation), the hat in this case was not the main lesson. It was merely a symbol of the power struggle that was taking place. By removing the hat (and asserting my authority to do so), I was able to take back and even out the balance of power that I had inadvertently given up earlier.

CHAPTER 4

Practical Prevention Strategies and Tactics

━━━━━━━━━ *In the previous chapter,* we presented tactics for helping moderators identify potentially problematic behavior early in the process. It is essential that moderators understand the sample source, screening and recruitment processes, and specifics of the invitation and incentive. Re-screening and meeting and greeting participants before they come into the discussion room are other key steps that can provide clues to potential problematic behavior.

In this chapter, the focus is on preventing problem behavior in the focus group room. As Goldman and McDonald emphasize: "One of the moderator's principal responsibilities is to provide a conversational environment in which participants feel free to express views with candor and sincerity." (Goldman and McDonald, page 79). The key issue is *how* to foster an open, safe environment for participants.

The development of rapport with participants is an essential art form for the moderator. This includes the moderator defining his or her role and expressing and describing in some detail the roles and behaviors that are expected of participants. Rapport building includes making the environment safe for all kinds of comments and accepting them from all kinds of people.

There are many elements to fostering an open and safe environment, starting with the tone and nature of the recruitment process. More directly, moderators can use carefully constructed introductory remarks to establish ground rules. These ground rules, along with the behavior that moderators model and the general messages moderators communicate with their non-verbal behavior, set the tone for productive focus groups. Keen awareness of potential problem behavior, gleaned from the tactics described in the previous chapter, can help moderators customize their introductory comments to prevent problems and establish a productive group dynamic.

There is often tension between the client and the moderator as to how long the introduction should be. Clients typically want to "get right at it" and to jump into the meat of the discussion very early. Moderators often seek a longer introductory and warm-up period, so that the group becomes "primed" for more productive and meaningful conversation later in the group.

As a general guideline, the moderator's introduction and the verbalization of ground rules should take no longer than five to seven minutes. Educating clients about the need for careful ground rule establishment and a warm-up period to establish rapport is another task the moderator must complete. Customize the ground rules depending on the nature of the topic and participants. Certainly, the tone and tactics used to foster an open and empathetic environment will be different for a group of cancer survivors discussing post-treatment support than for a group of NASCAR fans discussing their preferred consumer product. Moderators must carefully consider context and then use any clues or cues gleaned from the early identification tactics to customize their set-up and introduction.

Establishing Clear and Complete Ground Rules

Once recruitment and re-screening are complete and the moderator has done as much as is feasible within the circumstances to identify potential problem behavior, establishing clear and complete ground rules for the ensuing discussion is the next, and some might argue, most critical step.

FIGURE 4.1

Ten Problem Types: Prevention Part I

*Prevention Tactics of Four Types That Are **Always** Problems*

Example Ground Rules

Dominator	Cynic	Hostile	Intoxicated
"Everybody talks and nobody dominates. If you are a soft spoken or an outspoken person, your opinion is equally important to us. So if you are the kind of person who does all the talking, I may ask others to speak-up."	"Tell me honestly if you like or do not like something that I present. But please respect that others may have differing views. From time to time I may ask you to argue the other side of the story to make sure I gather a complete under-standing."	"I understand that some of you may be angry or concerned with some of the experiences you have had. I want to listen to everyone's experience, but I will put boundaries around how long we spend on any one person's concern."	• None. Intoxicated participants should be removed. • To dismiss: "Sam, please come with me." Escort from room and have the hostess arrange a safe way home for the Intoxicated • Or ask hostess to remove via "phone call"

Non-Verbal Cues to Help Prevent Problem Behavior

Dominator	Cynic	Hostile	Intoxicated
• During open-ended questioning make eye contact with anyone but the Dominator • Start around the table questioning with others, not Dominator • Position your body out of direct sight of Dom-inator	• Acknowledge Cynic both when arguing his or her point of view, but especially when arguing opposite position • Force the Cynic into an early role switch, to demonstrate desire for listening to all perspectives	• When describing ground rules, look directly at the Hostile when using the phrases above • When listening to the Hostile's story, be very attentive, make eye contact, acknowledge anger and emotion • Empathize	• When returning to the room, relax and show signs of relief, being ready to get to work—roll-up sleeves, take off coat, etc. • Use this opportunity of excusing the Intoxicated to build cohesion among remaining partici-pants

FIGURE 4.2A

Ten Problem Types: Prevention Part II

*Prevention Tactics of Six Types That Are **Sometimes** Problems*

Example Ground Rules

Wallflower	Follower	Co-Moderator
"Everybody talks and nobody dominates. If you are the kind of person who rarely contributes, I may call your name or find other ways to pull you into the discussion. I want to hear from everyone in relatively equal proportions."	"Try to hold onto your own opinion and do not be swayed too much by what others say. Remember that there are no right or wrong answers. We want to hear everyone's unique perspective."	"It's my job to ask the questions and try to keep the discussion on-track. I have some pretty specific areas to cover, so help me keep us focused."

Blatherer	Proselytizer	Joker
"We have a lot to cover today, so I will be the 'traffic cop' trying to keep the discussion moving. If I cut you off, please understand that I mean no disrespect, but am just trying to stay on topic so everyone has a chance to voice an opinion."	"There are no right or wrong answers in a focus group. If you agree with something someone else says, let me know. And if you disagree, that's OK, too. Let's respect the diversity of opinions."	"Focus groups can and usually are fun for the participants. But let's remember that we are dealing with a serious topic today, and let's limit the pranks."

Some aspects of the complete and clear moderator introduction are ethically demanded. The moderator must inform participants:

- They are being audio and video recorded (if, in fact, they are);

- Observers are watching (again, if this is true);

- Their comments will be held confidential (again, if this is true) and that there will be no attribution of their comments associated with their names;

- The focus group is strictly a research process and that there will be no attempt to sell anything in the group or as a result of the group.

FIGURE 4.2B

Ten Problem Types: Prevention Part II

*Prevention Tactics of Six Types That Are **Sometimes** Problems*

Non-Verbal Cues to Help Prevent Problem Behavior

Wallflower	Follower	Co-Moderator
• Early in the discussion, be sure to call on the Wallflower and attempt to engage • Be especially attentive and patient	• Early in the discussion, call on the Follower first and seek to get him/her involved	• When describing the ground rules, look directly at the Co-Moderator • Quickly assess if the Co-Moderator can be helpful to group dynamic—if so, seek to leverage

Blatherer	Proselytizer	Joker
• Set a quick pace to the discussion, especially early in the group • Communicate with pace setting that you will not allow for long, drawn out, off topic comments	• When describing the ground rules, look directly at the Proselytizer • As the group progresses, reinforce the unconditional positive regard for all	• When describing the ground rules, look directly at the Joker • Do not play along with pranks and jokes, and intervene immediately if joking becomes contagious

These basics should be communicated in every focus group, every time. Doing so reinforces respect for participants. Being entrusted with participants' opinions, beliefs, and attitudes is a sacred role.

It is often a good idea to state the purpose of the group and refer to the one or two key screening characteristics that make them a group. Describing screening requirements helps build bonds among the group by emphasizing the characteristics participants have in common. Brief purpose statements—in the participants' language, not marketing or other jargon—establish focus and parameters for limiting off-topic participant digressions.

The rest of the words the moderator uses to set-up the group discussion, establish the parameters, and lay out the ground rules are critical to the establishment of an ideal environment and the prevention of counter-productive behavior in the group. Below are some specific examples of ground rules that help prevent problem behavior.

Using Ground Rules to Foster a Productive Environment and Prevent Problems

Preventing and Minimizing Dominating Behavior

A critical step for every group and every moderator is to begin to establish rapport and trust with the focus group participants. This can be done as part of the explanation of the ground rules. Communicating that everyone's opinion is valued and that all are equal are good ways to show respect for participants. It also can be a way to prevent dominating behavior, as well as draw out Wallflowers.

One of the most important sentences to use to prevent dominating behavior is:

"Everyone talks and no one dominates."

Alternatively, and a little softer:

"We need to hear from everyone. So, please let us know your thoughts about every issue that comes up and make sure to leave time for everyone else to do the same."

In cases when a potential dominating behavior problem is identified early, it may be wise to add:

"Whether you are a soft spoken or outspoken person, your opinion is equally important to us."

If there certainly is a Dominator in the room for that session, look directly at the potential Dominator and say:

"So, if you are the kind of person who does all the talking in a

group session like this (continue eye contact, pause, and in a playful tone continue), then it is my job to make sure you don't."

If the tone and timing is right, this almost always generates a knowing, tension-relieving laugh from the participants. While the moderator has identified the Dominator, many or even all of the other participants in the room saw the problematic behavior coming as well.

Finally, in situations where there may be a Dominator and a Wallflower (or two), consider adding:

". . . and if you're the kind of person who does not usually say much in a group, I'll figure that out pretty quickly, and may try to pull you into the discussion."

Stating these ground rules accomplishes much all at once:

1. It establishes the parameters for appropriate focus group behavior.

2. In a non-threatening way, it lets the potential Dominator know that you know he or she is a Dominator.

3. It allows you to reference this ground rule later in the group if you need to bring the group back into focus by limiting the role of the Dominator.

4. It establishes the moderator's role with parameters for behavior that participants can expect from the moderator.

5. It gives the moderator "permission" to try to pull a Wallflower into the discussion.

While it is not necessary to use these exact phrases—and it is definitely preferable if the moderator customizes the phrasing to his or her own style—using a sentence or two with these basic sentiments will help foster a productive group dynamic.

Preventing Cynical Behavior

Are there clues that there is a Cynic in the group? Remember, the Cynic is negative toward everyone and everything. Here is a good ground rule to establish when the moderator suspects a Cynic is in the room:

> *"Give me your opinions in a straightforward and honest way. Tell me candidly if you like or do not like something that I present. But **please** (lots of emphasis) respect that others may have differing viewpoints. It is OK to disagree. From time to time, I may ask you to argue the other side of the story to make sure I gather a complete understanding."*

Similar to the first ground rule, this rule helps foster a productive group dynamic by communicating that it is acceptable to disagree and that everyone's opinions will be respected. Asking a Cynic to argue, just for argument's sake, the other side of the issue, is a key management tactic to diffuse the Cynic's all-encompassing negativity. (More description of this tactic is presented in Chapter 5). This ground rule gives the moderator permission to use this tactic later in the group, if needed.

Preventing and Managing Hostile Behavior

Hostile participants can be especially damaging to a group dynamic. Hostility is counter to fostering the open, safe environment that we seek to create as moderators. Often, truly Hostile participants will reveal themselves before the group even starts by seeking some type of corrective action from front-line personnel like the hostess. If this occurs, the moderator should be informed and should speak privately (if possible) and directly to the Hostile participant before the group starts.

Assuming that the moderator has identified the Hostile participant prior to the group discussion, and assuming that there is another person on-site capable of conducting a brief individual interview with a Hostile participant, take such participants aside and indicate the need and desire to gather their information in detail. Send the interviewer (a client, colleague, trusted facility manager) with the Hostile person to a separate area of the facility for a one-on-one interview. Provide the Hostile participant with an opportunity to share his or her story. Hostile participants often want acknowledgment and corrective action.

As a moderator, you are unlikely to be able to provide for the corrective action the Hostile participant seeks (money back from a service or product purchase, for example), but moderators or their surrogates can acknowledge that they have heard the Hostile participant's complaint. This alone often diffuses a difficult situation.

If this approach is not feasible or the Hostile participant has not been identified until the group begins, there are two general approaches to preventing the negative behavior from ruining the group discussion. With truly Hostile participants, preventing their rage is impossible, so the next best alternative is to put parameters around it so that the group is not derailed and other participants are not contaminated.

Typically, if there is a Hostile participant the moderator will know it very early in the group, and should use a ground rule like this:

"I understand that some of you may have concerns or may even be angry with the some of the experiences you have had. I want to listen to everyone's experience and opinion, but I will put boundaries around how long we spend on any one person's concern."

Approaches vary, but letting Hostile participants talk about their concerns early in the group often works well. Allow the participants to get their gripes "off their chests" and then focus the rest of the discussion on the objectives.

Failing to allow the Hostile participant to have his or her "say" early in the group often results in acting out and misbehaving during the remainder of the session. After Hostile participants have an opportunity to vent, the moderator has the right to use this as a way to pull them back into line if they begin telling their story again:

> *"Frank, you used your opportunity earlier to talk about your concerns; let's focus on . . ."*

Another less preferable alternative is to ask Hostile participants to hold their comments until the end of the group. This approach has the advantage of reducing the potential bias Hostile participants may have on the others in the group, but also increases the likelihood that Hostile participants' concerns will bleed through and color their comments on all of the other issues discussed in the group.

In any of these three approaches, non-verbal communication is important in effectively managing the Hostile participant. Through body language, the moderator should exhibit that he or she is especially attentive. Listen! Make eye contact, lean forward, take notes. Verbally repeat and summarize the Hostile participant's concerns to ensure accurate collection of the information, but also to fully acknowledge understanding and empathy.

Ultimately, handling the Hostile participant is a judgment call, one of the many that a moderator must make quickly. Yet these three approaches can all be used effectively depending on circumstance.

The worst (and a very common) decision is not to address the Hostile participant's concerns at all and simply try to go on with the group as planned. This nearly always has a counter-productive effect. A potential spin-off problem from the Hostile participant is that he or she becomes a Proselytizer and attempts to convince others in the group that due to his or her experiences, all the others should turn against the sponsor or concept as well. Clients typically are not keen on one participant contaminating all others' perceptions of the product, service, or concept.

Like Dominators, Cynics, and Intoxicated participants, Hostile participant behavior requires moderator intervention. Failing to address these types of problem behaviors in focus groups is all too common. All of these problem types (except Intoxicated behavior) can be managed into playing productive roles as productive participants.

Ground Rules and Intoxicated Behavior

The truly Intoxicated participant should be dismissed from the group, preferably even before participants are invited into the group discussion room. There are no ground rules that can prevent the Intoxicated participant's problem behavior. The only solution is to dismiss the participant. Again, preferably this is done prior to the group beginning. If not, and the Intoxicated participant is in the discussion room, simply say, *"Sam, grab your stuff and come with me please."* Escort the Intoxicated participant out of the room and turn over to a hostess or other support personnel to ensure the participant has a safe way home.

Basic rules of personal safety should be employed. Stay alert and calm. Do not let any of the Intoxicated participant's actions get under your skin. Deal with the Intoxicated participant quickly and unequivocally. Should you sense that he or she might become violent, call for assistance immediately.

While an Intoxicated participant can be embarrassing and a distraction, the moderator can use him or her to build cohesion among the remainder of the group. If the moderator noticed that the participant was intoxicated, it is likely that others did as well. They will be relieved that the problem behavior has been removed from the group. Use this to your advantage.

First, after dismissing the Intoxicated participant, return to the focus group room with a knowing smile and ready-to-work body language. Taking off your coat or rolling up your sleeves, for example, communicate that it is now time to get down to work.

Clever moderators may make comments like, *"Now that we are all here . . ."* or something else to communicate that the preliminary work (excusing the Intoxicated participant) is complete and the group is ready to work in earnest. Encouraging all participants to stay actively involved in the discussion may help disarm any fear that the dismissal of the Intoxicated participant created among the remaining participants.

Preventing the Wallflower

The same basic language used in the ground rule section to prevent dominating behavior also can be applied to the Wallflower (*see methods above*).

Preventing the Follower

Followers are common, and one way to prevent or reduce Following behavior is to use a line like this:

> *Try to hold to your own opinions and not be swayed too much by what others say. If you agree with something someone else says, fine, share it with the group. If not, and you disagree with something someone else says, share that with the group also.*

Preventing the Co-Moderator

If you sense you have a Co-Moderator, the following phrasing may be helpful:

> *It's my job to ask the questions and try to keep the discussion on-track. I have some pretty specific areas to cover, so help me keep us focused.*

Preventing the Blatherer

Blatherers are often particularly difficult to stop once they get going. If you sense you have one, try the following phrasing in your ground rules:

We have a lot to cover today, so I will act like a traffic cop trying to keep our discussion moving and focused. If I cut you off, please understand that I mean no disrespect, but am just trying to stay on topic and let all of you have a chance to voice your opinions.

Preventing the Proselytizer

Proselytizers are often particularly irritating to the moderator, client observers, and other participants. Use the following if you sense you have a Proselytizer in your midst:

There are no right or wrong answers in a focus group. If you agree with something someone else says, fine, share it with the group. If you disagree with something someone else says, share that with the group also. Let's respect the diversity of opinions.

Obviously, if you use every one of these lines in every introduction you will be speaking longer than the recommended five to seven minutes of introduction. Most experienced moderators have their basic introduction carefully constructed and have honed it over many iterations and for many years. Less experienced moderators may find the need to construct a standard introduction which covers all of the bases and then customize it with the phrasing above, incorporating one's own style and communication strengths. In either case, use these notions about prevention based on the information you have gathered through your use of the early identification tactics. These phrases also may be used at nearly any time if the moderator senses that problem behavior is occurring.

Pace Setting to Prevent Problems

Setting the appropriate pace is another technique to subtly communicate the desired behavior in a group. Pace can be set by the cadence of the moderator's speech in association with other non-verbal cues.

A quick pace can be established through asking short questions and expecting quick responses. This is especially valuable if you anticipate working with Blatherers or extreme Dominators.

At other times, a more reflective or inner-directed pace may be desired. Suggest short written assignments. Exercises and activities like collages, picture or image sorts, and a wide variety of other visual activities or exercises can be used to set the desired pace and prevent problem behavior.

Modeling Appropriate Focus Group Behavior

The moderator can communicate a lot about appropriate behavior through the introduction and verbal establishment of ground rules. Pace setting is a second key way to set the right tone. Finally, moderators can create productive environments through modeling some of the behaviors they want the participants to replicate.

- Use respectful words and tones.

- Listen attentively.

- Occasionally summarize what others say and ensure understanding.

- Occasionally, reveal something about yourself, especially during the introductions.

- Be "in the moment" by concentrating and focusing only on the task at hand.

- Do not interrupt (generally).

- Do not participate in sidebar discussions.

- Restrict notes from the back room and keep other interruptions to a minimum.

- Make an effort to pronounce participants' names carefully and use them as they prefer to be addressed.

- Be sensitive to culture and context in terms of addressing participants by first name or in more formal terms.

- Try to restrict irritating behaviors, like nail-chewing, table-tapping, and ice-chewing. Suggest to the hostess that potato chips and other noisy snacks are not appropriate for the focus group room.

Summary

Moderators have the fundamental responsibility to establish rapport with participants and foster an environment that permits free conversation of sometimes delicate and personal matters. At the same time, moderators must be able to sense or read their participants and establish themselves in the moderator role. Depending on context, cues, and circumstances, there are many approaches and lines that can be used to prevent problem behavior so that more meaningful information can be derived from the focus group.

The Rabbi

Hy Mariampolski, PhD
Qualidata Research Inc., New York, NY

THERE IS A SPECIAL KIND of dominant group participant that I like to call the "Rabbis." They can be of any religion, any color, bearded or clean-shaven, male or female. Rabbis tend to be on the elderly side, though age is not their primary qualification. What distinguishes Rabbis is their unassailable, recognized authority with respect to the subject under discussion.

Most dominant respondents come to group experiences with some degree of insecurity, anxiety, or arrogance. Consciously or unconsciously, they view the group discussion as an opportunity to dramatize themselves. Dominants may have pretensions of authority but, in reality, they are just loud, bombastic, and boastful. They behave competitively toward moderators and dismissively toward peers.

Rabbis are different. They may present themselves as shy and reserved or they can be as overbearing as any other type of dominant participant. What distinguishes them, however, is the behavior of other group participants, who become respectful, deferential, and even obsequious toward the Rabbi.

In the highly technical discussions I often lead among medical specialists and senior corporate executives, Rabbis appear without being announced. In a focus group of pediatricians conducted several years ago in New Jersey, their Rabbi had just published an important article in a leading medical journal. Group participants, several of whom were meeting him in the flesh for the first time, were eager to hear his opinions before rendering their own. Similarly, in an extended creativity group I conducted with optometrists in Los Angeles, it was not apparent until about midway into the session that the friendly gent to my right had been the teacher of almost every other participant in the group. That could not have been predicted from the participants' wide age distribution; some were about the same age as he, while one was at least twenty years younger.

Rabbis cannot always be identified at the recruitment stage; however, their agreement to participate may sometimes be used by recruiters to entice others to attend market research sessions. In a Connecticut focus group on an important new corporate management initiative, the CEOs, CFOs, and COOs in attendance were all eager to hear from the "brand name" CFO who was the draw for their own participation. They indeed were thinking through their own reactions to the new corporate policies being demanded by government authorities and wanted to explore alternatives valid for their own businesses. Like many encounters with a Rabbi in the group, the session was less an opportunity to hear various opinions than to observe the process of opinion formulation.

Backroom client reactions can vary widely. Sometimes they are as enchanted as everyone else in the front room. They may be tempted to tune out everyone but the superstar, while congratulating the qualitative research consultant and recruiter for obtaining the cooperation of someone with such a high degree of eminence. In one case, during a Silicon Valley session with telecom programming specialists, the clients called me to the back room to ask whether it would be ethical to offer a job to a group participant whose depth of knowledge and experience, amply demonstrated in the discussion, apparently qualified him for an open senior position with their R&D organization.

Often clients confuse Rabbis with conventional Dominators and incorrectly urge moderators to control or suppress their participation. This can be a very dangerous course to take because other participants may define the moderator's behavior as rude or ignorant. Besides, they may feel that the implicit social contract that impelled their own participation is being violated.

In point of fact, most often, client observers may miss what is going on completely because the Rabbi's influence is being exercised subtly through a wink, a raised eyebrow, and other facial gestures. Otherwise, participants may be unwilling to assert strong opinions until after the Rabbi has spoken. The best way to observe the Rabbi's effect is through the way it is reflected in others rather than through anything he or she does to exercise authority.

Culture may be the source of the roles Rabbis are playing. Many cultures maintain strong norms for appropriate authority behaviors in groups. Among Japanese respondents, for example, the most influential person in a focus group may be the quietest person sitting at the table, as I learned several years ago while interviewing the American divisional leadership of a major Japanese bank.

It also is wrong to assume that the Rabbi is never vulnerable to challenge. Sometimes, he or she may represent a particular school of thought or practice modality, subject to vociferous objections by those representing alternate points of view. In one of the earliest focus groups I ever conducted for a textbook publisher, during the 1970s, we had attracted a Rabbi, an eminent scholar, but also had recruited a dissident, championing a different theoretical position. Despite the adulation of several group members, the Rabbi did not have an easy time with the young rebel.

It is acceptable to check whether nonconformist viewpoints are present in the group, to invite their expression and to validate their importance.

The lesson demonstrated by the Rabbi is that, despite our best efforts, we cannot always hermetically seal group discussions from various authority relationships, cultural roles, and statuses that are brought into a session from the real world outside the laboratory. Even apparent peers have a natural pecking order, a structure of influence that they will bring to group experiences that moderators are trying to construct. Relations among group members are not always controllable, nor must we persist in struggling to be the ultimate power.

The focus group can be something different—not a controlled discussion in which the information marketers provide the critical variable structuring opinions. Instead, the group experience may be a snapshot of an ongoing set of relationships created before the session and persisting well afterwards. What we are witnessing in this context is an actual moment of influence in which ideas are being evaluated, processed, negotiated, and compromised.

If a Rabbi persistently changes people's minds in a focus group, it is not necessarily because he or she is exhibiting dominating behavior. Instead, we are viewing a pattern that is likely to occur outside the laboratory. In the real world, marketing communications always are filtered and processed by what Malcolm Gladwell's *The Tipping Point* refers to as "mavens"—experts, reference groups, and peer influencers that serve as the reality check for what people are hearing. People defer to authority figures in real life; opinions are crafted and evolve through an interactive process in which doubts become certainties, and information is turned into knowledge. When this process occurs in a focus group, we are viewing in microcosm an actual process of opinion formation and this should be welcomed, not discouraged.

How do we make sure that we are mobilizing the Rabbi's energy for the good of our group and to maximize the client's learning? Here are some ways for moderators and group leaders to stay ahead of a Rabbi.

Lessons Learned

1. **Acknowledgment.** It is hard to become a Rabbi, so they deserve recognition and respect. Mirroring your group's admiration helps you maintain rapport with everyone in the room. After two pediatricians referred to the article by that group's Rabbi, I suggested that he spend a few minutes describing its findings to everyone else in

the room. This gesture placed the entire group in a situation of equality. Afterwards, I probed whether knowledge about this study would change anyone's prescribing habits and solicited permission to mention that if anyone wanted to continue the discussion with the Rabbi, they could take time at the end of the official discussion.

2. **Leverage the Rabbi.** Turn the Rabbi's presence in the group into an opportunity to extend the client's insights into opinion formation. When it became obvious that participants in the senior executive study referenced above were deferring to the "brand name" CFO, with the agreement of my backroom client, we made his opinions the focus of the discussion. "Jim, you're the CFO of the largest company represented here and everyone, especially me, would like to hear what you are doing in response to the new law." We were then able to debrief everyone else in the room about the degree to which their own companies would be likely to make decisions in the same way.

3. **Humor.** Rabbis do not necessarily want to be the only voice heard in the room; they fall—usually reluctantly—into their old roles with respect to other participants. If your background and level of rapport are appropriate, you can defuse the situation with some gentle joking. As a former university professor myself, I was able to put everyone on an even footing in my optometrists group when I said, "What's going on here, haven't we all graduated? Dr. Horowitz, didn't you ever encourage class participation?" Everyone laughed in recognition and deferring to the Rabbi stopped being a problem.

4. **Projective and Enabling Techniques.** Exercises may be used to overcome the problems of different statuses in the room. All participants are on an equal level when they are reacting to unfamiliar stimuli. It is sometimes hard to implement projective tools with senior professionals and executives, but it is valuable to use them to overcome the "politeness barrier."

CHAPTER 5

Practical Management Strategies

▬▬▬▬▬▬ *In the previous two chapters,* strategies and tactics were outlined to identify potential problem behavior early in the process and ground-rule setting and other techniques to prevent problem behavior. These are important steps in creating a productive group dynamic, especially when the moderator has uncovered clues that suggest one or more participants may behave in ways that are counterproductive.

Should the early identification and prevention strategies fail to work, and surely sometimes they will fail for any moderator, it is incumbent on the professional moderator to be prepared. In this chapter, we present overarching strategies and associated tactics that can be customized to each situation to guide the moderator to quicker and more effective correction of problem behavior.

Moderating is an art form. None of the suggestions and ideas offered will work if the moderator is in any way insincere or unauthentic. True insight comes from fully and completely listening and observing, and this is most effectively done when participants are treated with genuine respect. More than any of the strategies described below, respectful treatment (what Carl Rogers refers to as "Unconditional Positive Regard"*) is a prerequisite for managing problem behavior.

** See **On Becoming a Person: A Therapist's View of Psychotherapy, 1961.***

Individual moderators need to uncover their strengths and use them in the development of a style that works for their clients, their participants, and themselves. Through study, experience, experimentation, and peer coaching, moderators can develop specific non-verbal cues, phrasing, and tone of corrections that work best for them. Think of the following strategies as a series of structures, like unfinished homes, that moderators can customize to their specific needs, tastes, and the specific focus group content and context.

The first and most broadly applicable of these strategies is the Problem Behavior Correction Continuum (Kahle, 2004). The Problem Behavior Correction Continuum is based on the realization that sometimes, perhaps often, the cure can be worse than the condition. Critical to managing problem behavior is ensuring that all others in the group remain engaged and no one's opinions, including the Dominator or other problem participants, are repressed by the moderator's corrective actions.

In the second part of this chapter, three more corrective structures are presented—forced role switching, in-group dyads and triads, and visual and written feedback exercises—that can be used when the moderator encounters the specific problem behaviors described in Chapter 2. A summary list of "dos and don'ts" for managing problem behavior is provided. The chapter concludes with a description of how a moderator can sometimes employ a Co-Moderator productively and a description of how to make the Dominator the moderator's ally.

The Problem Behavior Correction Continuum

Inexperienced or anxious moderators frequently make the mistake of not identifying problem behavior early enough to correct it. Another challenge for moderators is to prevent problem behavior in the focus group room before it happens, especially when the moderator has so much else to manage.

A common mistake moderators make when they encounter problem behavior is to over-correct. Krueger (1988) cautions: "Most important, be tactful because harsh and critical comments may curtail spontaneity from others in the group." Similarly, Langer writes, "Being abrupt with a respondent during his or her first or second remark can send the wrong message to other group members: 'You better be cautious or I'll do the same to you.'" (2003).

When moderators are so firm and direct in their corrections that some of the respondents are stifled, the "cure" becomes worse than the condition. Thus, the trick is for moderators to intervene just enough to correct the problem behavior, but not so much that they intimidate participants into silence or suggest that only responses that please the moderator are acceptable. Like good referees in a ball game, effective moderators keep the participants playing within the rules; yet, they do not seek to influence the outcome.

One strategy is to use the Problem Behavior Correction Continuum (Figure 5.1). This concept suggests the moderator begins with the mildest form of non-verbal corrections and then proceeds to firmer and more direct verbal corrections until the behavior is corrected. In this way, the moderator reduces the risk of stifling ideas and opinions from others, while kindly, gently, and incrementally increasing correction intensity and directness, until the behavior is contained and managed. This approach of mild to firm, indirect to direct, and non-verbal to verbal, can significantly help manage counterproductive behavior without overly influencing the outcome of the group.

Perhaps the simplest and mildest form of non-verbal correction is simply avoiding eye contact with the problem respondent, especially at the point when the moderator has completed a question and is expecting responses from the group. If this does not work and the Dominator or other problem type continues, try moving to the next level of correction by positioning away from direct sight of the Dominator. Stand to the side of the table, facing opposite the Dominator, or even turn slightly to appear to be addressing only others in the group. If the dominant behavior persists, become more direct and firm with non-verbal corrections and begin using verbal corrections.

FIGURE 5.1

Problem Behavior Correction Continuum

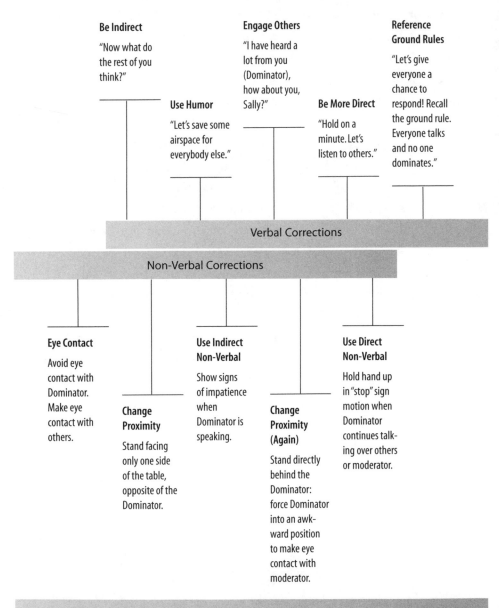

The mildest verbal correction is a simple redirection, *"Now what does everyone else think?"* Similar to the non-verbal corrections, continuing to move along the continuum until the corrections begin to work will allow the moderator to correct counterproductive behavior while minimizing the risk of stifling the group. Move to the next degree of correction only when needed.

Finally, if the corrections are still not working, the moderator, if the ground rules have been carefully established, can always reference the ground rules and ask for compliance. *"Let's give everyone a chance to respond. Recall the key ground rule 'everyone talks and nobody dominates.'"*

Dominators exhibit one common type of problem behavior in focus groups and the Correction Continuum is quickly and easily applicable to the challenges they present to the group and the moderator. Some of the other types can be corrected using the same basic strategy of corrections, especially the Blatherer, the Joker, and the Co-Moderator.

Many moderators have great difficulty cutting participants off. Blatherers, especially if they are kind-hearted and well-intended, even if off base and extraordinarily long-winded, are a genuine problem for many moderators. When a true Blatherer is encountered, the Correction Continuum works well for both the moderator and the group.

The moderator can work through a set of prepared non-verbal and verbal corrections, from mild to firm, from indirect to direct. If indirect and non-verbal approaches do not ease the problems of a Blatherer, the moderator ultimately needs to learn how to cut him or her off. *"Thanks, but I am afraid I have to cut you off and let someone else speak now. Remember the ground rules, 'everyone talks.'"* In some cases, the gentle and indirect approach will work so that the moderator does not need to be so firm. But if ground rules have been set appropriately, the moderator has been given permission to cut off the long-winded and off-topic participant.

The Joker also can be especially problematic for some moderators as joking can become contagious and affect the entire group dynamic. Often, it is unclear how far Jokers will go with their incessant attempts at humor. A light-hearted, playful, and humorous tone is often productive for a focus group. So how does the moderator effectively manage the Joker without raining on the parade? The moderator should gently and incrementally use corrections until the problematic behavior is contained, following the basic rules of the Correction Continuum.

Co-Moderators also can be corrected with a similar mild to firm, indirect to direct approach. If these initial approaches do not work, consider using humor in response to the Co-Moderator taking over. Try, *"Hey, they pay ME to do this,"* or, *"Want to change seats?"* Tone is everything in these situations and each moderator needs to develop a personal style that is most effective. Following the basic rules of the Correction Continuum can help nearly every moderator. It is a useful, malleable conceptual structure that all moderators can use to fit their own circumstances.

Forced Role Switching: Participants Taking on the Role of the "Other"

Empathy is the ability to perceive situations and circumstances from the point of view of someone else. Being empathetic is a critical way all humans learn how to interact successfully, as it allows one to anticipate the behavior of another, as well as to have one's own behavior anticipated and predicted. Empathy is a key ingredient that allows us to make sense of a confusing world. We have all heard phrases like "walking in someone else's shoes" or "putting on another hat." These common expressions reflect an interactive element that makes all of us human and civil. George Herbert Mead was the sociologist who introduced empathy as important to understanding human interaction. He also introduced concepts like the "significant other." Coser's summary below captures one dimension of the importance of empathy to the focus group:

> George Herbert Mead maintained that the experience of role-play and pretense in early childhood were vital for the formation of a mature sense of self, which may only be achieved by the child learning to take on the role of the other, i.e., seeing things from another person's perspective. By doing this, the child may eventually be able to visualize the intentions and expectations of others and see him or herself from not just another's point of view but from groups of others. The generalized other represents the common standpoints of those groups.   *(Coser, 1977)*

In the same way that children need to learn to view things from the "other's" perspective in order to mature and develop a self-identity, focus group participants, especially those who are causing problems for the group, can be forced to switch roles so that their behavior is not counterproductive.

Jean Bystedt, Siri Lynn and Deborah Potts, in their delightfully practical and genuinely instructive book called *Moderating to the Max* (2003), include a full chapter that asks participants to explore different perspectives. They describe "word bubble" exercises where different roles are presented and participants are asked to fill in the words that they might say if they were in these various roles. Similarly, Bystedt et al describe, "hats," a commonly used exercise where the participants are asked to "put on a different hat than you usually wear." Finally, they describe "the debate." This self-explanatory exercise is where the group is arbitrarily split in two and then asked to argue, sequentially, both the pros and cons of an issue, product or service. The debate is an especially useful exercise when there is a need to fully elicit a broad range of perspectives on an issue. Read *Moderating to the Max* and try these techniques in your focus groups.

Critical for using these techniques to manage problem behavior is to keep key exercises "in your back pocket" to spontaneously use upon encountering Cynics, Followers, or Proselytizers. Hostile participants also can be redirected sometimes by using these types of exercises where the moderator forces the participants into the role of the "other."

For example, some Hostile participants can be transformed into productive participants by being asked, *"If you were in the role of the company representative, what would you do to make your situation right?"* This approach can change a Hostile participant's angry tone into a thoughtful, productive group asset. Hostile participants turn into articulate voices of constructive criticism when asked this type of question. Many times they will quickly change their tone and wonder why no one has ever asked them this before.

Cynics, Followers, and Proselytizers all share the common trait that they cannot, or choose not, to see the world from the "other's" perspective. Cynics think it is all hogwash. Followers do not usually want to think at all, but rather, just mimic others. Proselytizers believe their perspective is clearly the only right one and cannot imagine that another perspective can be right or true. By gently encouraging (OK, sometimes forcing) these problem types to see things from another viewpoint, the moderator can start to break down the narrow views that fuel their counterproductive behavior. Think of it as taking a toy train off the tracks and sending it in the other direction. Same train, same tracks, just a radical change in direction.

Even when these exercises are not pre-planned and designed into the guide, the moderator can use these and other variations of forced role switching to help spontaneously manage problem behavior in focus groups so that more meaningful information is derived.

Break It Up: In-Group Dyads and Triads

When confronted with extreme Wallflowers, extreme Followers, or even ineffective Co-Moderators, another correction strategy, or structure, is to break the larger focus group down into smaller groups. This can work when moderating particularly shy participants, dealing with sensitive issues, or for some reason, the moderator just cannot seem to get the participants to open up and communicate at a deeper level. These smaller groups can be pre-planned or implemented spontaneously, depending on the situation and context.

There are many variations, but at its most basic, the moderator suggests exercises to be conducted within smaller groups of maybe two or three participants. Following brief (less than ten minutes usually) dyad or triad discussions, one of the participants from each dyad or triad can report out the essential elements of each discussion or exercise.

The critical benefit of these approaches is that the moderator makes the discussion safer by reducing the number of participants directly listening. Some participants will be more open, more talkative, and as a result, contribute more to the group process. This is obviously one method of seeking more input from Wallflowers. It also can force Followers to relay their own opinions, rather than just mimic others. In order for this approach to be most effective, however, the moderator needs to group people carefully so that the ensuing dyad or triad is most productive. For example, better to put two Followers together than a Follower and a Dominator. Putting like types together is a good general rule.

These small group approaches also have disadvantages. Time in the dyad or triad should be carefully limited. One reason is that it will be difficult for observers to follow the action when there are two, three, or more small groups working simultaneously. Observers may see these exercises as an opportunity to take a break and stop listening. Another key disadvantage is that the small group discussions are unlikely to be clearly captured on audio and videotape, thus making the "report out" portion of the exercise critical. Third, truly extreme counterproductive behavior may continue, even in the small group, without moderator intervention.

Still, using dyads and triads in focus groups—especially for warming up shy participants (Wallflowers), seeking original input from Followers, and reducing the distraction and time wasted by a Blatherer—can be effective in managing these problem behaviors for more meaningful moderation of the focus group.

Put It on Paper: Written and Other Visual Exercises

There are many good reasons to use written and visual exercises in focus groups. Written exercises can be done individually so that no one participant unduly influences the others. Some participants are likely to be more comfortable with visual expression rather than oral, so asking them to contribute in writing or via other visual methods can be especially productive. Visual and written exercises can add another dimension to "talk-only" focus groups. Written and visual exercises can be designed to address client objectives and make the group more dynamic for participants and clients. This same set of exercises, viewed through another prism, can be used to manage problem behavior.

Moderating to the Max (Bystedt et al, 2003) is an excellent reference for understanding and learning about some of the various written and visual exercises that are commonly found in experienced moderators' toolboxes.

At its most basic, written feedback can be obtained by asking each participant to write down a few words of reaction, before the group discusses a concept, package, tag-line, etc. Quite simply, instruct the

participants to write on a tablet before each portion of the group discussion begins. Asking participants to read and explain their answers
is a way to limit the intimidation effect that a Dominator may have
on the rest of the group, at least the first time around the table. This
simple written approach also can reduce the effect of a Cynic's negativity and the often-offensive dogmatism of the Proselytizer.

There are many visual and written exercises with multiple variations and permutations of each. "Perceptual mapping" techniques in
focus groups, during which participants are asked to place a concept
along a one or two-dimensional continuum, can be instructive. The
follow-up questioning about why they perceive a product is equally,
if not more important, than the visual data collected. This technique
can be used effectively to diminish the negative effects of Dominators,
Cynics, and Proselytizers.

There are other visual exercises that do not require the participant
to write. One alternative to use, especially when a strong Dominator
is present, is the "voting dot game." Simply provide participants with
a series of self-sticking dots (available in multiple colors at nearly any
office supply store) and ask them to place the dots next to their most
liked, least preferred, or any other attribute one seeks to measure.
These voting games have risk, as inexperienced or politically motivated clients may add up the dots in order to claim, "see my concept
won 49 to 36 dots!"

The dot game can be used to assess the relative strength of a concept or product vis-à-vis others tested in the group. The relative diversity of opinion also can be assessed in this way, thus limiting the
contaminating effect of a Dominator, Cynic, or Proselytizer. A variation is to provide two more colors of dots and ask participants to
place the green ones on the notes or stimulus to represent "likes," and
the red ones to represent "dislikes."

The bottom line is that each moderator should have a set of tools
ready for nearly any situation. Written and visual exercises deployed

both spontaneously and as pre-planned exercises, can go a long way to diminishing the negative effects of Dominators, Cynics, and Proselytizers. A summary of the tools covered so far appears in Figure 5.2.

FIGURE 5.2

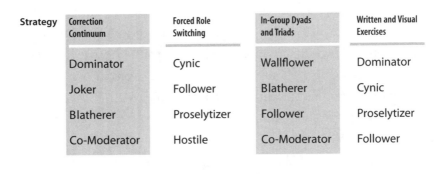

Four Corrective Strategies and Problem Participant Behaviors
They Can Help Manage

Strategy	Correction Continuum	Forced Role Switching	In-Group Dyads and Triads	Written and Visual Exercises
	Dominator	Cynic	Wallflower	Dominator
	Joker	Follower	Blatherer	Cynic
	Blatherer	Proselytizer	Follower	Proselytizer
	Co-Moderator	Hostile	Co-Moderator	Follower

Dos and Don'ts of Managing Problem Behavior

There are many techniques and tactics that come "naturally" for some moderators. For seasoned moderators, a set of responses and non-verbal cues seem obvious and intuitive. Fortunately, some other writers, notably Langer, Mariampolski, and Krueger have published these. Figure 5.3 is a summary and compilation of these three authors' suggestions for managing problem behavior, placed in the context of the Problem Participant Behavior Typology. These dos and don'ts apply to all of the four strategies described above.

Co-Moderators: A Special Case

So far in this chapter, four strategies or structures that moderators can customize to the specific type of problem behavior encountered and the overall context of the focus group have been presented. The various strategies are applicable and most effective with certain problem

FIGURE 5.3

Dos and Don'ts of Managing Problem Behavior in Focus Groups

Dos of Managing Focus Groups	Don'ts of Managing Focus Groups
Do use body language and hand gestures to support your verbal communication. (Langer)	Do not lose your patience. (Mariampolski) This is likely the first focus group experience for many of your respondents. Give them time to learn to behave appropriately.
Do withhold or limit eye contact from Dominators and Blatherers. (Langer)	Do not condemn or shame anyone. (Mariampolski) There are many other alternatives to managing problems in groups.
Do playback or summarize participant comments— especially good for Hostile participants and Blatherers. (Langer)	Do not become a problem yourself, by displaying anger, hostility or cynicism. (Mariampolski) It sets the wrong tone and models inappropriate behavior.
Do "inadvertently" interrupt Blatherers, Dominators and Cynics— "Oh, I am sorry ..." (Langer)	Do not threaten to eject or threaten to withhold the incentive. (Mariampolski) Threats create the wrong tone.
Do note that you have heard repeated statements before—"Yes, you mentioned that before." Especially good for Blatherers, Dominators and Followers. (Langer)	Do not overcorrect, especially early in the group. Even the slightest harsh tone can stifle others. (Krueger, Langer)
Do delayed response—"Let's start with someone else this time ..." Especially good for Dominators and Cynics. (Langer)	Do not make or communicate judgments about respondent comments. Try to use value neutral gestures and responses. (Krueger)
Do move right along— "I need to cut in here." Especially good for Blatherers and Dominators. (Langer)	Do not create problems for yourself. Asking participants to reveal education, affluence or social/political influence, especially early in the group introductions, will allow Dominators a way to claim superiority. (Krueger)

types of behavior. However, Co-Moderators are a special case, because their presence can sometimes be especially effective.

First, the moderator needs to assess his or her Co-Moderating participants' effectiveness at moderation. Are the Co-Moderator's probes on the money, allowing for the same (or even more) information emerging if the moderator had asked a similar question? Is the Co-Moderator including everyone in the discussion and not playing favorites? Is the Co-Moderator helping to make a productive group, consistent with client objectives?

If the answers to all of these questions are "yes," then the confident moderator should sit back and listen. These self-managed groups can be very productive and the group can take on a life of its own, becoming very revealing. In many cases the Co-Moderator can be allowed to continue playing this role with no negative and, indeed, a very positive effect on the group.

On the other hand, some Co-Moderators do not fully comprehend the objectives of the group. This can cause them to ask inappropriate or irrelevant questions. Just like the official moderator, the Co-Moderator may not be attentive to all participants nor the overall group dynamic. In some cases, the Co-Moderator may just not be a very good questioner or manager of a group of people. If some aspect of this second set of circumstances occurs, then the moderator must take some corrective action to reign in the Co-Moderator, just like with the other problem types. The key difference with the Co-Moderator is that he or she can *sometimes* be a moderator's asset.

Making the Dominator the Moderator's Ally *

* This section is a slightly revised excerpt of an article "Managing and Leveraging Dominant Participants" that originally appeared in **QRCA Views**, Fall 2004, Volume 3, Number 1.

Accepting that some respondents are going to exhibit dominant behavior at least some of the time suggests that we should not only learn to manage it, but leverage it when possible. Dominance is a matter of degree. So the accomplished moderator can learn to manage dominant behavior and use it to the benefit of the group dynamic and ultimately as an advantage.

One way to use a Dominator to the group's advantage is to set up his or her point of view as a marker with which others can safely agree or disagree. For example, if a Dominator speaks out strongly against the product-positioning concept because of *a, b,* and *c,* the moderator can re-position the comments by restating them without the Dominator's harsh tone, excessive volume, or self-appointed expert stance.

Once the moderator has disentangled the dominating behavior from the ideas that appear to be dominant, the moderator can begin to assess the degree to which these arguments are persuasive to the rest of the group. If the group remains persuaded after the moderator reinforces the safety of agreement or disagreement with the Dominator's ideas *a, b,* and *c,* this is a finding, not solely a problem group dynamic.

Since Dominators are often very bright, quick-witted, articulate, and persuasive, using this approach can leverage the best characteristics of the Dominator to assist in fully achieving client objectives.

Summary

Four strategies, or structures, have been presented in this chapter as guides for the moderator to use when encountering specific types of problem behavior, as described in Chapter 2. The Problem Behavior Correction Continuum is a key conceptual tool, a structure which moderators can use to more quickly and more effectively manage problem behavior in focus groups. Guard against overcorrecting by managing with mild to firm, indirect to direct, and non-verbal to verbal corrections. Over correction can potentially stifle spontaneity or influence the ideas and opinions of others in the group, making the consequences of the "cure" worse than the condition.

Other strategies for dealing with counterproductive behavior include forcing the participants to take on the role of the other, breaking the focus group down into smaller groups (dyads or triads), and using written or other visual forms of feedback. Choose and use the various strategies based on the type, variety, and degree of problem behaviors encountered in each specific focus group situation as summarized in Figure 5.2.

Advanced moderators can even leverage Dominators to their advantage, by disentangling the Dominator's bluster from his or her main points. By repositioning the key points to the remaining participants devoid of the "know-it-all" tone, the moderator and his or her client can see if these main points still resonate.

The Intoxicated Doctor

Elyse Dumach

Elyse Dumach Consulting, Chicago, IL

IT WAS 1985 and I was thrilled to be in Marina Del Ray, California conducting a series of focus groups with doctors—then, a new type of participant but one that was critical to my pharmaceutical client. While I've moderated hundreds of doctor groups since then, I'll never forget this encounter with intoxicated behavior.

In those days, we didn't yet have "best practices" for research with doctors. We were still figuring out the best ways to recruit and provide incentives that actually would motivate physicians to show up. To get them to come, we would offer a nice meal ordered from a great restaurant, along with drinks, in addition to a monetary incentive.

Just about everyone in this memorable group was fine, except for one of the doctors who showed up already a little tipsy. He continued to imbibe, and not just a little too much, but *far* too much and he soon became slobbering drunk. It was a problem that was troubling the rest of my participants as well. I tried to control him in the room, but it was impossible, and there was no way he was going to sober up soon. My mind was in overdrive wondering, "What do I do?"

Fortunately, it was obvious to my clients in the back room that both his behavior and the situation were only getting worse as the group |wore on. Thank goodness one of my clients came into the room to let the boisterous drunk doctor know that he had an urgent phone call (there were no cell phones in those days). Once the Intoxicated participant was out of the room, the client arranged for a taxi to take him home and get his car back to him the next day. It was quite an ordeal and the entire episode distracted us from fully meeting the client's objectives for this group.

I was so lucky that my clients and the other participants were understanding and even had a sense of humor about it. Some of the other doctors even joked with me to ask if they would be the next to go. This lighthearted concern is one of the problems with excusing a participant—others fear they may be next and ideas may be stifled.

If I had it to do over again, I would have been more sensitive to the doctor's "state of mind" when he arrived. I should have sent him home when I noted he was tipsy and before he ever set foot in the focus group room.

Lesson Learned

Participants who arrive at the focus group intoxicated are unlikely to improve as the group proceeds. Identify problem behavior early in the process and take immediate steps to prevent the Intoxicated participant from contaminating the group.

> **Note:** Today, it would be highly unlikely and not recommended that alcohol be served at a focus group (taste tests aside). In either the front or the back room, alcohol and focus groups do not mix. Still, some facilities serve beer and wine and have stocked refrigerators for clients.

"Feel," The Joker

Robert W. Kahle, PhD
Kahle Research Solutions Inc., Lakeside, MI

I WAS IN ATLANTA conducting focus groups for a high-tech company, a long-time client. One respondent arrived late. He was a 50ish "hometown Atlanta boy," as he described himself. He entered the room shortly after I began welcoming the participants and establishing ground rules. He did not have a table name tent. I had an extra on the table and a marker and asked him his name so I could make him a table tent like the other participants.

"OK," he said, "my name is spelled *F*," I wrote *F*. "*E*," I wrote *E*. "*E, L*," he concluded as I completed the name table tent. "Feel?" I said. "Yes sir, that's how we need to spell it so you Yankees can pronounce it right. My momma always called me 'Philip,' but all my friends call me *F-e-e-l*," (in an exaggerated southern drawl).

The room exploded in laughter. I was caught off-guard, as I was most concerned with the aggressive set of objectives these clients were expecting us to achieve. But I went along and laughed heartily with everyone else. I admitted the obvious. I was raised in Ohio and acknowledged my Midwestern accent. I played along, and tried to be helpful by offering that maybe "Feel" could translate if anyone was having trouble understanding my accent. I quickly continued into my introductory remarks and went about moderating the group. I did not change the spelling on his name card (a mistake).

Within the first five minutes of discussion, "Feel" had cracked several more jokes about my accent. Within a few more minutes another one of the participants joined in, and soon thereafter, rather than a focus group exploring a new high-tech concept, it began to look more like a "make fun of the moderator's accent" focus group. For the next two hours, despite my attempts to play along, casually dissuade the group from telling more jokes, and ultimately becoming stern and serious, the participants, with "Feel" the Joker leading the way, interjected some accent related barb into the discussion so frequently it became a problem. The entire group process had become an opportunity for joking around. For the next two hours we heard more "Feel" jokes than one could ever imagine. "Feel's" joking was contagious.

Lessons Learned

1. Play along with Jokers, but only to the degree that you do not hand over control of the serious nature of the group.

2. Be cautious when the moderator becomes the butt of the jokes. This can cause a "you/us" dynamic rather than a "we" dynamic.

3. When joking becomes contagious and overbearing, steps need to be taken to bring things into a serious light focusing on achieving client objectives. Try "forced role switching" or moving to written or other visual types of exercises in order to regain focus and control.

CHAPTER 6

Practical Strategies Considering Culture and Mode

Qualitative research is practiced all over the world. Major international qualitative projects conducted in multiple countries and cultures have become common for international marketers. So far, this book has focused on problem behavior and practical strategies for managing meaningful focus groups from an American perspective. In the United States there are multiple ethnic groups and distinct cultures. Ethnic pluralism is common in many countries. Understanding focus group practices across cultures can be productive and helpful for the moderator who works in multiple cultures in one country as well as for those who conduct projects internationally.

Our society's diversity and cultural variation begs several questions. Do the ten types of problem behaviors fit across cultures? Do some cultures or groups define problem behavior differently? Do the correction strategies work across all cultures or are they culturally specific?

Unfortunately, due to the proprietary nature of most qualitative marketing research, very little evidence about cultural similarities and differences in thinking about problem behavior exists. There are few mentions in published literature about cultural variations with problem behavior in focus groups.

To begin to address the issues related to culture and appropriate focus group practices, and as part of the Qualitative Research Consultants Association's (QRCA) 2006 Annual Conference, a panel of

international research experts was convened to explore problem
behavior across culture. The report of this panel discussion forms the
first part of this chapter.

The second part of this chapter examines issues related to research
mode. Over the last two decades, new forms of qualitative research
have developed and are now commonly employed. There are many
variations but online focus groups and telephone focus groups are two
commonly employed techniques that differ in significant ways from
conventional face-to-face focus groups. In this section, some differences in types of problem behaviors encountered across these methods and variations in the application of the corrective strategies are
explored.

Everybody Talks, Nobody Dominates

The primary objective of the panel discussion "Everybody Talks and
Nobody Dominates: Practical Strategies Considering Culture and Context" was to create a heightened awareness and understanding of the
role of culture on perceptions of problem behavior and application of
the correction and management strategies across various ethnic and
cultural groups.

The four panelists who participated are all experienced qualitative
researchers with decades of combined experience. All have conducted
international projects and all are highly respected Qualitative Research
Consultants. The four panelists were:

- J. Robert Harris, JRH Marketing Services, New York
- Peter Lovett, Consumer Profile Group, Thame, Oxfordshire,
  U.K.
- Ricardo Lopez, Hispanic Research Inc., East Brunswick,
  New Jersey
- Jane Gwilliam, Global Coordinator, Research International–
  The Qualitative Space, London

The first issue the panel addressed was the degree to which the Typology fits across cultures. Do moderators encounter these ten types of behaviors when moderating focus groups among specific ethnic groups in the U.S. or in other countries?

The general consensus among the panelists is that moderators encounter all of the ten types of behaviors in most cultures, but there are variations in frequency and intensity. Peter Lovett sums up the feelings of the panelists succinctly:

"Yes, I agree with the others. I think the Typology is applicable across multiple cultures, but I also think it is a matter of degree. So, a Dominator may not appear as dominant in some cultures as in other cultures."

The panelists were careful not to generalize, but some patterns of behavior by ethnic group emerged. For example, some Latino groups are prone to being especially polite, sometimes to a fault, according to Ricardo Lopez. Yet this behavior depends on many factors, not solely ethnicity. Age, geographic residence, length of time in the U.S., degree of assimilation, and the specific context of the focus group are all important factors to take into account, the panel stressed. Lopez provided this example:

"(The Typology) sort of fits. I do research with the U.S. Hispanic market, a very difficult thing to do because we are talking about many, many different cultures coming together and being in a very different culture than in their country of origin. It is not that the types are that different, we just see them in greater or lesser degrees. For example, the Cuban community in Miami, they went through a lot of issues, especially those who left Cuba during the revolution. There are a lot of Cynics. You are doing the group, and you have a lot of people who have things to say. There also are cultural issues; for example, Cubans feel at home when everyone is talking at the same time. Is that a problem behavior?

Not necessarily. But if I tell them not to do it, the group does not work. It dies."

Lopez expands on his key point that the U.S. Latino market is really made up of many cultures and that country of origin is important to understand. His experiences with focus group participants from the Dominican Republic reiterate the point.

"If you are talking to Dominicans, they tend to talk a lot. They tend to be the Blatherer types. I call them my Dominican Philosophers. But it is not just culture, it is age, length of time in the U.S., and it really depends on a lot of factors."

Similar to Ricardo Lopez' perspective, Jane Gwilliam believes the Typology fits across cultures, but emphasizes that age can be especially important within a culture. As an example, she cites Asian participants acting deferential to the elder in the group, leading to Follower behavior. She comments:

"Yes, I think these types exist everywhere. My experience crosses Latin America, Asia Pacific, and particularly Sub-Saharan Africa. In Asian cultures there is a much tighter range on age or seniority, so you get the younger deferring to the older (acting like a "Follower"). One method of dealing with this is to recruit with homogeneity of age or seniority, so you reduce the amount of "Follower" (or deferential) behavior. Still, we are totally dependent on the local moderator to interpret cultural nuances."

Along these same lines, Lopez provides more examples of various types of problem behavior occurring more often or less often in the U.S. Latino groups he moderates. He emphasizes understanding context, especially language and country of origin.

"Another issue we have is when someone is being very quiet (like the Wallflower). It depends on the country of origin too. In Central America and Mexico, they are taught to respect the

leader. I am in a position of authority and they see me almost as a professor, sometimes. They are respecting me. They are going to be quiet and they are going to let me talk. I really have to break that down because they are being too polite!

"Similarly, here in the U.S., I have to do bilingual groups and some participants may speak better in English and others in Spanish. If one person prefers English and the discussion is in Spanish, even though they understand everything, they are afraid they may not speak as fluently so they appear as a Wallflower. When I switch to English, all of a sudden they come to life, and they can be the Dominator then."

Early Identification and Prevention

Two key approaches to managing problem behavior are identifying it early and preventing it by the way the group is treated and informed about the process. Specifically, how do recruitment strategies vary by culture? What lessons can be learned from other cultures about early identification and prevention approaches that can be implemented in North America? Are there differences by culture and context in terms of effective ground rules?

The panel generally responded that there are significant differences in recruiting procedures across cultures, as well as differences in ground rules. Clearly there are lessons that can be learned in American marketing research recruitment practices from colleagues in the U.K.

In contrast to client-provided list recruiting or recruiting from facility databases or panels, as is common in the United States, researchers in the United Kingdom often use recruiters who are local to an area and who host the group in their homes. Jane Gwilliam explains:

"We do not have panels in the U.K., except for special uses. What we have are recruiters who go around in their own home areas and invite people to come to the groups. In my company (Research

International), sixty to seventy percent of the groups are con-
ducted in recruiters' homes. There are good and bad things about
this. The worst thing is 'bent' (dishonest) recruiters. We also have
'bent respondents.' But with the really good recruiters, you tend to
get fresh respondents, a lot more virgins, never been to groups
before. I believe this is completely different than what happens in
most other countries. In Australia, they do some recruiting door-
to-door. In India, in rural areas, obviously it is face-to-face, door-
to-door.

    "The other advantage of the in-person recruiting is that the
recruiter can observe behavior and identify problem respondents.
For example, a recruiter might say to me. 'She (the potential par-
ticipant) was perfect, but God could she talk.' As a result, the
recruiter can alert the moderator to a potential problem. It also is
cheaper to do homework assignments, because the recruiter can
just give the participant the materials right there."

The closer bond created with in-person recruiting is something
that can be important when recruiting Latino focus groups. Lopez
points out that there is great variation in the U.S. Hispanic markets
and suggests that traditional telephone recruiting of Latinos may not
work as well as some may assume.

    "Our politeness can be a problem. We will say 'yes' we are coming
to a focus group over the phone. We have no intention whatsoever
of coming to the focus group. In person-to-person it works better
because of the way we connect with each other. Recruit Latinos
face-to-face and there is a lot better chance they'll show-up."

These comments were followed by a brief discussion of ground
rules. Lopez explains that the ground rules many American moderators traditionally use may not work with Latino groups. Imposing
ground rules on a Latino group may not have the desired affect of an
orderly, yet creative, focus group.

"We are not structured people. Ground rules are scary. Do not structure us. We are not structured. We speak by storytelling. So a lot of times I ask a question and the response may be people talking and talking and talking and going on. Their response is in there. We go here. We go there. We go on tangents. But you have to listen for the response. Ground rules like talk one at a time, or nobody dominates, may constrain us."

For any ethnic focus group, as opposed to general market group, participants are likely to want to understand why the research sponsor is interested in that specific group. This context may make participants curious and inquisitive about the research objectives, sponsor, and process.

Bob Harris acknowledges that the Typology fits across cultures, but emphasizes that the context of the group may cause individuals to play specific roles that some find problematic. Rather than any inherent behavioral trait associated with culture, the role-playing that moderators observe is due to context, not necessarily any negative intent by the participant exhibiting the problem behavior. Harris comments:

"Specific to African-Americans and probably Latino groups as well. . . . A lot of times people fall into a type based on the specific situation they are put into. For example, with a lot of African-American groups, you will get people at the beginning and they want to know 'Who is doing this? Why are we here? Why is this whole group black? Is the company that is doing this group white, like a major corporation? Who is sitting behind the mirror? Why are they there? Are there any black people back there? And why do they care what black people think?' and on and on.

"So some people may become Dominators or may become troublemakers because of the situation they have been put in and they are unsure of what is happening. So you really have to be careful at the beginning to be sensitive to a situation where it is

obviously an ethnic recruit and it is pretty clear at the beginning that the idea is to get an ethnic perspective. You need to tell them what it is all about. You have to be sensitive enough and tell them enough to get the comfort level to the point where they say what they really feel.

"In some ethnic focus groups, sometimes one or more people in the group will feel it is their responsibility to interpret what people are saying from an ethnic point of view. So, instead of stating their (personal) point of view, they say 'black people feel this way,' or, 'African Americans feel that way.' They may become the Co-Moderator or the Dominator and you need to be sensitive to that and that it is created because of the circumstance we put them in."

Building on this concern, the panelists emphasized that recruitment method and specifications may affect the results. Imposing the moderator's or the clients' cultural biases onto a group, either in the recruitment structure or in the moderation approach, can lead to misunderstanding. Jane Gwilliam relays this useful story:

"In the U.K., we rarely separate people by ethnic group. We are all integrated and that is the way we usually do groups. Sometimes we are too sensitive in how we categorize people. For example, we had a U.S. client that worked with dolls and they wanted to talk with little English girls about their dolls. So the girls were to bring their dolls with them and then we were going to expose them to some other (client created) dolls. Six nine-year-old girls walked in with their little dolls. Four were white, one was black, and one was Asian (broadly representative of the diversity in the area we were working). And the client is having the "heebie-jee-bies" in the backroom because they would have separated the kids by ethnic origin and shown the black kids black dolls and the Asian kids Asian dolls. And they could not understand why the

kids were not carrying ethnically-correct dolls. They were all car-rying white dolls because that is how my culture is. (The clients did perceive this as a problem at first, but not after we had a thor-ough discussion about ethnic relations in the U.K.). Ultimately they saw this as a finding that the ethnicity of the dolls was important to the client, but not the little girls."

Peter Lovett provides another example of challenges with recruit-ment specifications in the U.K.:

"I recently did some work in Northern Ireland. I don't want to be sectarian, so we recruit both Protestants and Catholics for the same group. On every functional level, the group discussion works, people talk and are polite. But even the first names imme-diately tell everyone if you are Catholic or Protestant. The area you live in, tells everyone immediately if you are a Catholic or a Protestant. As soon as you have any symbol, identifying color, or reference, it suddenly screams out the historical relationships in Northern Ireland. They continue to be polite and discuss the topic, but the mood is not the same. So now, no matter the topic, I recruit Catholics and Protestants for separate groups in Northern Ireland."

Management Strategies

Earlier in this book, four management strategies were explained that can be employed when experiencing various types of counterproduc-tive behavior in focus groups. These are the use of The Correction Continuum, forced role switching, in-group dyads and triads, and written and visual exercises.

The panelists defined some additional interesting strategies that can work well in various circumstances. Jane Gwilliam explains that being part of a culture that is different from the participants' cul-ture can be used to an advantage. She describes how she takes on the role of "naïve outsider" in situations where she is not a part of the culture.

"I have moderated groups in the U.S. with an American researcher in the backroom, so I can say "I am a foreigner, tell me what you mean?" It is a really good projective and then I have the Americans in the backroom to help me understand the meaning of their comments."

This strategy can be employed in many situations, like a male moderating a group of females (or vice versa), a Caucasian moderating a group of African Americans, or any circumstance where the moderator is clearly different than the participants. Taking the role of the "naïve outsider" is a powerful strategy to grow a group dynamic that might be problematic into a revealing and productive session.

Similarly, Ricardo Lopez describes how he becomes the "devil's advocate" in his U.S. Latino groups in order to manage Dominating, Following, and Proselytizing participants. This approach can be used regardless of culture to manage these problematic behaviors.

"One strategy I use all of the time is devil's advocate. One thing about Latino groups is that everyone seeks to be polite and then they group think. 'Oh yeah! We love it,' and they don't. If everyone is following along with a Dominator or a Proselytizer, I take a position opposite and I become the one debating this person. I see if the rest of the group is going to go with me, or the other way. If they stick with the other position, then that's a finding. So playing devil's advocate can work well in those situations which are common in Latino groups."

Bob Harris takes a different approach. His perspective is that the correction strategies to use are more a function of the style and approach of the moderator rather than any behaviors associated with a specific culture of participants.

"My personal feeling is that the way you handle problem behavior in a group is more related to my personal moderating style than any ethnic differences. I would handle people pretty much the same way across ethnic groups. You do want to have respect for everybody, all the time."

Still, Harris points out that in his experience, African-American groups can be especially sensitive to language issues:

"In African-American groups and ethnic groups generally, there is a lot of sensitivity about how well or poorly they speak. If they have an accent or use a lot of slang, because of the way they speak and what they say, if they will be perceived by other people in the group or the people behind the mirror as less well-educated. Sometimes people are a little sensitive to how and what they say is interpreted by others."

Gwilliam directly addresses the question of the application of the four management strategies across culture:

"Yes, all of the first three management approaches (Correction Continuum, forced role switching, and in-group dyads and triads) work across cultures. But the last, visual and written exercises, is culturally specific. So what I do when developing protocol for international studies is give a range of different exercises so the moderator can pick out the most culturally sensitive. Northern Europeans are much better at rational things like ratings and rankings. Southern Europeans are much better at the visual and more psychological, projective exercises."

Finally, the panelists agree that there are "Universal Truths" that apply across cultures. There are human commonalities, regardless of culture and context. It does not mean a lack of sensitivity to culture and context, but that basic approaches like being genuine and sincere and communicating openly in a transparent way work everywhere.

Specifically, treating each participant with unconditional positive regard, asking for and giving mutual respect to all participants, assuring confidentiality and adhering to standard ethical requirements, such as informing the participants of recording devices being used or observers being present, and refraining from selling the product or service in the group, apply across all cultures the panel members have encountered.

This panel discussion was an important step in understanding problem participant behavior across cultures. The panelists' generous contributions of time and insight will provide professional moderators enhanced sensitivity and heightened awareness of cultural variation in problem behavior in focus groups and methods to effectively manage these dynamics.

Practical Strategies Considering Research Mode

Most commonly when the term *focus group* is used, the traditional in-person or face-to-face focus group comes to mind. Typically, but not always, focus groups are held in facilities that have large conference tables in one room with a one-way mirror where observers can see and hear the proceedings while in the back room. Commonly, the discussion is recorded and a moderator's guide is used to provide some structure to the discussion. While there are many variations, the basic elements of a focus group are:

- Participants have some common bond or characteristic;
- Participants will be or have been exposed to the same stimulus (using a particular product or seeing a particular commercial, for example);
- The session is recorded and/or observed;
- A professional moderator, trained in managing group dynamics and interpreting the data that results, conducts the session;

- The discussion has a focus and there are clearly articulated objectives;
- There is no attempt to sell products or services to the participants, only to understand perceptions, attitudes, values, and behaviors.

Since development of the traditional focus group in the late 1950s, two additional qualitative research modes have developed that are now commonly used. These are the telephone focus group and the online focus group. Telephone focus groups were invented in the late 1960s, and while this is the dominant methodology for some types of work (pharmaceutical, agricultural), the method is less well-known to clients and practitioners working in other industries or in other product or service categories. Recently, the development of "white boards" and other online meeting software have allowed for showing stimulus (both static and video) while on the phone with participants. Telephone focus groups have now become computer-aided or technologically enhanced.

Telephone Focus Groups

More than a simple conference call, the telephone focus group is best operated when there is technical assistance. Conference calling facilities supply an online link that allows the moderator to see a list of the participants' names on the screen and lights flash when each participant speaks. This allows the moderator to "see" who is speaking to assist in managing the conversation flow. Additionally, moderators can have one or more online chat sessions open, so they can communicate with the technician and/or client observers while simultaneously moderating the discussion via the phone. The second aspect that makes telephone focus groups different than a conference call is that they are often done "full duplex"—everyone can speak at once and there is no clipping by one participant cutting off another.

Online Focus Groups

Online focus groups, coinciding with the "dot com" boom of the mid-to-late 1990s, enjoyed a fad-like quality for at least a couple of years. Today, the online focus group is generally perceived as a mainstream research methodology, one that adds to the toolbox of qualitative researchers, but does not displace face-to-face or telephone-based methods. Online focus groups are best used with participants who are comfortable communicating online, and for topics related to the online world.

There are two major forms of online qualitative research with groups, the synchronous version (chat style), during which a group of participants responds to the moderator and hopefully interacts with each other at the same time. The other general approach is the asynchronous message board or bulletin board style group. These typically last from three to ten days, and allow for participants to respond at their leisure to questions typed in by a moderator.

Like so much in qualitative research, solid data are not available on the number of classic face-to-face groups that are conducted compared with telephone or online methods. Both telephone and online methods are now widely practiced. George Silverman, a pioneer in the use of the telephone focus group, estimates that there are at least "a couple of thousand" telephone focus groups done each year.* There are many variations of each primary mode of conducting group depth interviews, each with its own particular advantages and disadvantages. Most relevant to this book though, is the frequency of problem behavior and the variation in the nature of problem participant behavior, and correction approaches by mode of qualitative group depth interviews. A full review of the strengths, weaknesses, and appropriate applications of each of these research modes is beyond the scope of this book.

*See the website of Market Navigation (www.mnav.com) for articles by telephone focus group–inventor George Silverman, "A Comparison of Face-to-Face Focus Groups, Telephone Focus Groups, and Online Focus Groups."

The Frequency and Nature of Problem Behavior Across Research Mode

In researching this portion of the book and speaking with many moderators who use both telephone and online methods, the general consensus is that moderators encounter problem participant behavior less frequently when conducing focus groups online or via the phone compared with face-to-face. Some advocates of both methods argue that their preferred method is superior because of less problem behavior for the moderator to manage and the client to endure. Caution is needed, however, to disentangle sales and marketing efforts regarding these techniques from clear, documented, dispassionate empirical comparisons.

Many online moderators report that they have no problem behavior and never have encountered any problems with participant behavior in the online world. Casey Sweet, an experienced online moderator, comments in an article* that for online versus traditional methods, the moderator has less domination to manage.

*See "Designing and Conducting Virtual Focus Groups" by Casey Sweet in **Qualitative Market Research: An International Journal,** June 2001 special issue "Research in Cyberspace," pages 130–135.*

"One interesting and overall difference online is that it is much more difficult for someone to dominate the group. An overbearing respondent does not have the same power or influence with words in the dialogue stream. All respondents are composing their responses simultaneously and not waiting for others to respond. The online environment can create a more even playing field and can mitigate other influencing factors such as gender, age, ethnicity, accents, physical appearance, and shyness, not to mention the weather."

Similarly, in a book edited by Miller and Walkowski, Sweet alludes to problems with Blatherers and says in the online focus group environment "long-winded responses do not take up precious time."

Accepting this at face value then, the Dominator, Blatherer, and even the shy Wallflower appear less often in online groups. Dominating behavior in a face-to-face group session often is evident by the Dominator being the first to answer or using a dismissive tone in relation to other participants. In the online focus group, tone is not an issue. In the case of the most popular form of online focus groups—the bulletin board style—responses are asynchronous, so these behaviors are not evident in the same way as in face-to-face sessions or telephone focus group sessions.

Similarly, it seems obvious that it is easier to ignore the long and off-topic typing of a Blatherer compared with the vocalization of the same sentiment in a face-to-face group setting. While it is difficult and unlikely that a participant in a face-to-face focus group can fully tune-out a Blatherer, it is easy to conceive that those who type a lot more into the bulletin board can simply have their responses ignored by other participants. Some participants blather out of nervousness, and this seems to be true for vocal blathering but not for written or typed blathering.

Critics might argue that encountering fewer problem behaviors in online group sessions is due to so little group interaction in that environment. The absence of problem behavior also reflects an absence of the extreme expressions of support or disgust that are impossible to conceal in a face-to-face environment.

Still, proponents of this methodology argue that absence of problem behavior is an inherent advantage of online methods. Telephone focus group advocates report some problems, similar to traditional face-to-face groups, but also suggest that there are inherent advantages to the telephone group compared with online or face-to-face.

Generally, it seems that telephone groups provide for a more focused environment where bad behavior is more difficult because communication is more constrained (people are accustomed to speaking one at a time on the phone) and structured than in a face-to-face focus group. George Silverman writes:

"(It is) much easier to control dominators in telephone groups because people are more easily interruptible ... (You can) kick someone out of group privately and invisibly."

Silverman goes on to express the thought that telephone groups are a natural setting for participants, more so for many than online or in what some perceive to be sterile focus group facilities. Perhaps most important is that telephone groups allow for anonymity (as do most online groups) and this makes participants more at ease and less likely to behave badly. Silverman tells a classic story of the openness of physicians participating in telephone focus groups.

"During telephone focus groups, we discovered that physicians are willing to discuss how they have killed people by using inappropriately high dosages of medications, how they have treated patients incorrectly, how they have cut corners from accepted practices, and where they are uncomfortable with gaps in their knowledge."

While there is mention of the Dominator and Blatherer in some of the published literature about these alternative types, there is scant evidence in these and only anecdotal stories about moderator's experiences with other types. George Balch and Lynne Doner describe an example of the Proselytizer misbehaving in a telephone focus group (*see page 45*). But for the other types—the Cynic, Hostile, Intoxicated, and the rest—there is little, if any, mention of these types appearing in online or telephone focus groups.

Practical Strategies Considering Research Mode

Recall that four general strategies or structures are provided for moderators to use when considering how to manage problem participant behaviors. These are:

1. The Correction Continuum

2. Forced Role Switching

3. In-Group Dyads and Triads

4. Written and Visual Exercises

Are these strategies equally effective across the three primary modes of conducting qualitative research? Are there other strategies that are more appropriate for addressing and managing problem behaviors in online and telephone focus groups?

Conceptually, the Correction Continuum, designed with face-to-face groups in mind, can still be effectively applied with telephone and online groups. If problem behavior occurs in online groups, the same basic soft to firm correction approach will work. An online moderator can begin by gently requesting (individually or as part of the group) a participant to stay on topic, or to respect all other participants' perspectives and then move to reiterating ground rules, and all the steps in between, if needed. This can apply in both the chat style and bulletin board-style online focus group. However, in the online and telephone focus group environments, since there is only written (online) or verbal (telephone) communication, the approach of starting with non-verbal cues and working to verbal instructions does not hold.

One of the key methods of communicating desired and appropriate behavior in an in-person setting is body language and other non-verbal cues that a moderator can both receive and send. Receiving helps the moderator understand the participants' behavior, and sending helps the participants understand the expectations of the moderator and redirect behavior contrary to the group objectives. The absence of visual cues results in a loss of data and also removes one key communication tool of the moderator to effectively manage problem behavior. These are disadvantages of both online and telephone modes of qualitative research.

In telephone focus groups, the moderator can use tone of voice and cadence to move from mildly directive to very directive to maintain appropriate decorum in the group. In the telephone focus group, unlike online but similar to face-to-face, open-ended questions can be asked with no designation of the participant who is to answer first. In this way, the Dominator can emerge by being the first to answer in the telephone focus group situation.

In the telephone focus group (at least those that are technician-supported) there is the ability to mute specific participants' lines. This is a correction strategy that can be used when a moderator encounters a difficult participant, but does not want to excuse him from the group. To implement, the moderator simply sends a note to the technician to mute the dominating participant's line, until being called on by the moderator. In this way, the participant behaving badly will get the message, without potentially stifling other members of the group, as they are typically unaware of the Dominating participant's line having been muted.

Breaking the group down into several smaller groups of two or three participants (dyads or triads) is another strategy used to manage counterproductive behavior in the focus group. This basic strategy is applicable in technician-aided telephone focus group environments, where subgroups of participants can be sectioned off from other subgroups so they can have small group conversations before being brought back together in the full group setting.

This can be implemented with each subgroup working simultaneously, and not being provided the mechanism to listen to the other subgroups; it may be implemented sequentially, with each subgroup being able to listen, but not heard while the other subgroup confers. These techniques and variations work well to limit the problems caused by Dominators, Cynics, Proselytizers, Wallflowers, and Followers. The telephone focus group technology truly does provide advantages for the moderator and ultimately the client.

In online groups, the moderator can suppress comments by any or all of the participants so that only selected participants see the comments of others. This is another technological advantage of online groups. It is especially useful when there is a participant behaving badly in the group and contaminating others. The moderator can simply suppress the comments from the problem participant so others do not see it.

The third general strategy, forced role switching, can work in all three modes. Examples of using forced role switching include asking participants to wear another "hat" or take the role of the "other" (a company representative, a dissatisfied consumer, etc.). Debates can be set up in either the online or telephone modes easily, and some might argue, with greater effect, than in the face-to-face environment.

The last strategy, using written or other visual exercises works best in person. However, new techniques are being developed for online groups where participants can post visuals like image collages, digital pictures, video diaries, and other digital voice or image data on websites as part of their research experience. This type of activity can provide great depth and texture to a research exercise, but currently is being used by only a few researchers.

As digital audio and video recordings can now be easily posted to the websites or streamed over the Internet, the future will see a merging of online and telephone focus groups. As consumers become more comfortable with these digital devices and more accustomed to sharing digital data on the Internet, focus groups will become multimedia experiences for both participants and observers.

Summary

This chapter explored problem participant behavior across culture and research mode. While the Typology generally fits across cultures, there are certainly variations in the frequency and intensity of the problem behavior in various cultures. Similarly, there is variation in the frequency of problem behavior across research modes. Both telephone and online modes of conducting focus groups provide additional, technologically enhanced methods of managing problem behavior.

Hostile Participants

Robert W. Kahle, PhD

Kahle Research Solutions, Inc., Lakeside, MI

IT WAS 2002 and I was working as a subcontactor to one of the big quantitative research suppliers serving the auto industry. This was a large qualitative project that I and about a dozen other moderators had been involved with for several years. The goal of the project was to talk with customers of auto dealerships for a luxury brand of a large auto manufacturer to understand satisfaction with dealer sales and service practices.

The quantitative supplier had just hired new personnel to operate the recruitment and logistical aspects of this major study. In a cost containment effort, they decided to recruit via mail and email, alerting all of the dealership's customers about the focus groups, the incentive, and asking them to call if they were interested in participating. Let's just say that screening was less of a priority than filling the groups quickly and inexpensively. This recruitment approach generated a self-selected sample.

As this particular dealership was located in a small city in Michigan, formerly home to manufacturing plants that had closed during one of the auto industry's contractions, most everyone in the area worked for, formerly worked for, or had some connection with the auto manufacturer who was the client. The group was held in a Holiday Inn with an adjoining room receiving a closed circuit video and audio feed so that dealership management could observe the group. Several attended, enjoying the deli tray and soda, while watching the group on a 27-inch television.

I knew I was going to be in for a long evening as I greeted the first respondent to arrive and he was clearly angry about "the lemon" he had purchased. He asked if a representative from the manufacturer was going to be there because he wanted his money back, not a little bit of money because of a bad service experience, but the entire $50,000 he had spent on the "car of his dreams." He carried with him a satchel of letters, service repair orders, and other documents related to his claims. I told him I wanted to hear his story and I would listen carefully once the group began, but that the purpose of the group was to talk about sales and service practices at the dealership, and not the mechanical or engineering aspects of the vehicle itself. He sat down, pulled out his stack of paperwork, and looked ready to fight.

As other participants began to arrive, I started to get really nervous because most of them carried stacks of paperwork as well as the angry, combative demeanor of the first participant. To make a long story short, several of the participants had active "lemon law" claims against the manufacturer and the others were just plain angry. Their degree of hostility varied, but all carried stories to tell, along with their documents. Some talked strictly about the vehicle, despite my efforts to keep them focused on dealership practices. Some talked about their problems with the dealership staff itself, while still others integrated comments about the financial or personal repercussions of the manufacturer's decisions and the larger economic impact on the city. Nearly all wanted some form of compensation for their problems well beyond the $100 focus group incentive they were promised. I did my best to follow the focus group guide and get the participants to comment on the topics of interest to my client. Yet nearly every comment was laced with hostility, anger, and resentment.

When the group mercifully ended two hours later, it was clear that part of the story was the vehicle's mechanical problems, but another aspect was the economic dislocation so many felt as a result of the manufacturer's plant closings. It was also equally clear that there was a problem with the way the group was recruited.

Lessons Learned

Hostile participants, especially when you have many in one group, should be screened so that the moderator and client are aware of the reasons for their anger before the group begins and decisions can be made about whether the participation will be productive. Be extremely cautious with self-selected samples.

Another key lesson is that Hostile respondents will sometimes "show their hand" very early, often upon arrival at the facility, by asking for correction of their problem or compensation from front-line personnel (the hostess). Frequently, they will carry documentation—letters, repair orders, legal documents, etc.—to support their claims.

A final lesson learned is that the truly Hostile respondent cannot (and should not) be contained. Let Hostile participants tell their stories early in the group. Put limits on their time, and then move on to the rest of the group and redirect their energy to address the client objectives. Attempting to contain the Hostile participant often will result in contamination of the entire group.

References

Balch, G. I., and D. M. Mertens (1999). "Focus Group Design and Group Dynamics: Lessons from Deaf and Hard of Hearing Participants." *American Journal of Evaluation*, 20(2), 265–277.

Balch, G., J. R. Harris, R. W. Kahle, G. Silverman, and The Professionalism Committee of the Qualitative Research Consultants Association (2003). *Professional Competencies of Qualitative Research Consultants*. Camden, TN: QRCA.

Bystedt, J., S. Lynn, and D. Potts (2003). *Moderating to the Max: A Full-Tilt Guide to Creative, Insightful Focus Groups and Depth Interviews*. Ithaca, NY: Paramount Market Publishing, Inc.

Coser, L. (1977). *Masters of Sociological Thought: Ideas in Historical and Social Context*. New York: Harcourt Brace Jovanovich.

Goldman, A. E., and S. McDonald Schwartz (1987). *The Group Depth Interview: Principles and Practices*. Englewood Cliffs, NJ: Prentice Hall.

Kahle, R. W. (2004). "Managing and Leveraging Dominant Focus Group Respondents." *QRCA Views*, 3(1), 34–38.

Kolkebeck, N., R. D. Lorinchak, A. Martin, M. A. Shugoll, K. Smith, and C. Tompkins (1999). "You Get What You Asked For." Glastonbury, CT: Market Research Association, Qualitative Research Consultants Association Joint Task Force.

Krueger, R. A., and M. A. Casey, (2000). *Focus Groups: A Practical Guide for Applied Research*. Thousand Oaks, CA: Sage Publications, Inc.

Langer, J. (2001). *The Mirrored Window: Focus Groups from the Moderator's Point of View*. Ithaca, NY: Paramount Market Publishing, Inc.

Mariampolski, H. (2001). *Qualitative Market Research: A Comprehensive Guide.* Thousand Oaks, CA: Sage Publications, Inc.

Merton, R. K., M. Fiske, and P. L. Kendall (1956). *The Focused Interview: A Manual of Problems and Procedures.* Glencoe, IL: Free Press.

Miller, T. W., and J. Walkowski, (eds.). (2004). *Qualitative Research Online.* Madison, WI: Research Publishers LLC.

Murphy, A. (2006). "The Wild, Wild West." *QRCA Connections,* August 2006, 5(6). Retrieved September 15, 2006 from *http://www.qrca.org*

Rogers, C. (1961). *On Becoming a Person: A Therapist's View of Psychotherapy.* Boston: Houghton Mifflin.

Silverman, G. (2003). *A Comparison Between Face-to-Face vs. Telephone vs. Online Focus Groups.* Market Navigation, Inc. Retrieved September 15, 2006 from *http://www.mnav.com/onlinetablesort.htm*

Silverman, G. (2005). *Introduction to Telephone Focus Groups.* Market Navigation, Inc. Retrieved September 15, 2006 from *http://www.mnav.com/ phonefoc.htm*

Stewart, D. W., and P. N. Shamdasani (1990). *Focus Groups: Theory and Practice.* Thousand Oaks, CA: Sage Publications, Inc.

Sweet, C. (2001). "Designing and Conducting Virtual Focus Groups." *Qualitative Market Research: An International Journal,* 4(3), 130–135.

Wells, W. D. (1974). "Group Interviewing." In *Handbook of Marketing Research,* R. Ferber (ed.), 133–146. New York: McGraw Hill.

About the Author

Robert W. Kahle, PhD

Bob Kahle is a sociologist and qualitative research expert who conducts focus groups and individual depth interviews in person at facilities nationwide and virtually, using the latest technology and research tools to uncover critical input from customers, suppliers and thought leaders. Bob has worked for Fortune 50 manufacturers and service providers, as well as non-profit and governmental organizations tackling tough social problems.

With more than two decades of research experience, Bob has moderated thousands of focus groups, trained aspiring moderators, and conducted intensive workshops to hone the skills of both experienced and new focus group moderators.

Kahle Research Solutions (KRS), founded in 1994, is built on Bob's solid academic foundation, and fortified with an unwavering commitment to integrity, analytical depth, timeliness, and responsiveness to client needs. KRS balances methodological rigor with real-world practicalities on each project it undertakes.

In addition to his PhD from Wayne State University, Bob earned MA and BA degrees in Sociology from Ohio University in Athens, Ohio.

Learn more at *www.KahleResearch.com*

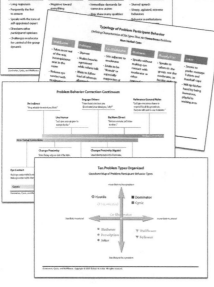

The Moderator's Tool Kit

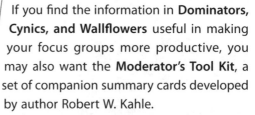

If you find the information in **Dominators, Cynics, and Wallflowers** useful in making your focus groups more productive, you may also want the **Moderator's Tool Kit**, a set of companion summary cards developed by author Robert W. Kahle.

This set of six heavy-duty cards packaged in a handy storage envelope summarizes the practical strategies discussed in the book. It's ideal to help moderators remind themselves of various strategies and tactics to moderate more meaningful focus groups.

The Tool Kit also is an excellent resource to help explain to clients how and why you used certain strategies to cope with problems in the focus group room. Focus group facility directors will want these handy cards to train front-line personnel about how to recognize problems during the screening and re-screening processes.

The color-coded cards include an organizational chart of the Typology, a summary of the correction continuum, and summaries of prevention tactics and language that can be included in moderators' introductions to set the stage for meaningful focus groups.

At a glance you can identify the information you need to help get your focus group back on track or deal with a problem without disrupting the entire group.

The Tool Kit is available only from Paramount Market Publishing. You can order today online at www.paramountbooks.com, by calling toll-free 1-888-787-8100, by faxing 607-275-8101 or send $15, which includes shipping, to

Paramount Market Publishing, Inc.
950 Danby Road, Suite 136
Ithaca, NY 14850.

Call us for quantity pricing on **Dominators, Cynics, and Wallflowers,** and on **The Moderator's Tool Kit.**